"THE COVID-19 PANDEMIC, INDIA & THE WORLD"

DR ABHILASHA S BYAKOD

INTRODUCTION

Coronavirus disease 2019 (COVID-19), the highly contagious viral illness caused by severe acute respiratory syndrome coronavirus 2 (SARS-CoV-2), which is a single-stranded RNA with protein spike, envelope membrane, and nucleic capsid. In most of the cases, the average incubation period is of 4–14 days.[1] It has a catastrophic effect on the world's demographics resulting in more than 3.8 million deaths worldwide, emerging as the most consequential global health crisis since the era of the influenza pandemic of 1918. Like other RNA viruses, SARS-CoV-2, while adapting to their new human hosts, is prone to genetic evolution with the development of mutations over time, resulting in mutant variants that may have different characteristics than its ancestral strains. Several variants of SARS-CoV-2 has been described during the course of this pandemic, among which only a few are considered variants of concern (VOCs) by the WHO, gives the impact on global public health.[2]

Dentists work in an environment of aerosol and splatter. The airborne material can spread at a distance of eighteen-inches from the operator site. To protect the dental community, the Centers for Disease Control and Prevention, ADA, and World Health Organization published guidance for oral health care providers on how to control the spread of the disease.[3] Centre of Disease Control (CDC) issued interim guidelines besides following the standard precautions which urged dental practitioners to postpone elective procedures, surgeries, non-urgent dental visits, and to contact the patient before the initial visit. The Indian Dental Association (IDA) and Indian Endodontic Society in a joint position statement strongly recommended that a dental practitioner should not treat a patient in his/her dental office UNLESS they can comply with the emergency preparedness checklist. This checklist includes disinfection and sterilization protocol, personal protective equipment (PPE) including N95 face masks, face shields, and protective outerwear.This advisory also stated those patients only requiring emergency care should be considered for treatment in a well-equipped dental clinic adopting strict protective measures; rest all patients should be tele-consulted, managed pharmacologically and scheduled for the care later on priority once the regular dental services are restored.[4]

The pandemic has resulted in the loss of livelihoods due to prolonged shutdowns, which have a rippling effect on the global economy. Even though substantial progress in clinical research has led to a better understanding of SARS-CoV-2 and the management of COVID-19, limiting the continuing spread of this virus and its variants has become an issue of increasing concern, as SARS-CoV-2 continues to wreak havoc across the world, with many countries enduring a second or third wave of outbreaks of this viral illness attributed mainly due to the emergence of mutant variants of the virus.[2]

Despite the unprecedented speed of vaccine development against the prevention of COVID-19 and robust global mass vaccination efforts, the emergence of these new SARS-CoV-2 variants threatens to overturn the significant progress made so far in limiting the spread of this viral illness.[2]

History & Origin of SARS-CoV-2

The influence of viruses and viral infections on human history has been broadly described by the social history of viruses ever since the modifications in human behavior during the Neolithic period around 12,000 years ago. This was the period when humans began to expand their agricultural communities and an exponential increase in the spread of viruses leading to becoming endemic was observed the most. With the rapid globalization and anthropogenic activities with time, pathogenic transmission has escalated across the globe and resulted in viral pandemics. It was the mid-19th century that was remarkably known for pathogenic viral outbreaks and their multiplex associations with humans and animal species. This further leads to cross-species transmission, posing a high threat to human health and well-being.

Later at the beginning of the 21st century, it was observed that due to the rapid globalization and human activities, pathogenic transmission across continents has escalated and resulted in several pandemics, especially viral pandemics. The pandemic caused by old diseases, namely plague, cholera, and yellow fever in addition to some emerging diseases such as Ebola, Zika, severe acute respiratory syndrome (SARS), middle east respiratory syndrome (MERS), and COVID-19, makes it the most ferocious century in human history. As per the reports, these viral pandemics have caused significant mortalities and majorly affected the international economy over the last three decades.[5]

Until 2003, barely two human CoV(HCoV) strains, HcoV-OC43 and HcoV-229E, were recognized, but from 2003 to 2021, the world has experienced havoc and an exponential increase in mortality rates due to the emergence of 5 other deadly strains of coronaviruses: HcoV-NL63, HcoV-HKU1, severe acute respiratory syndrome coronavirus (SARS-CoV), middle east respiratory syndrome coronavirus (MERS-CoV), and SARS-CoV-2, which may cause fatal respiratory infections in humans.

Now the biggest threat that the world is facing today is the outbreak of novel coronavirus (COVID-19) that originated in Wuhan, Hubei Province, China, in December 2019 and rapidly spread over the rest of the world in a short time. As a result, the World Health Organization.

(WHO) in February 2020 has named it coronavirus disease 2019, abbreviated as COVID-19, and on March 11, 2020, the situation was declared a pandemic.It can best be characterized by pneumonia-like symptoms that may further extend up to major hypoxia and several cardiovascular complications. Coronaviruses are enveloped, positive-sense, single-stranded RNA viruses belonging to the Coronaviridae family and a leading cause of acute respiratory, hepatic, and neurological diseases with variable severities in vertebrates. They are referred to be the common human pathogens with the tendencies of fleeting recombination and mutation. It is due to the presence of crown-like spikes on the periphery of these viruses, popularly called coronaviruses.[5]

Like other RNA viruses, SARS-CoV-2, while adapting to their new human hosts, is prone to genetic evolution with the development of mutations over time, resulting in mutant variants that may have different characteristics than its ancestral strains. Several variants of SARS-CoV-2 have been described during the course of this pandemic, among which only a few are considered variants of concern (VOCs) by the WHO, given their impact on global public health. Based on the recent epidemiological update by the WHO, four variants of concern (VOC) SARSCoV-2 have been identified between December 2020-May 2021

1)alpha coronavirus (B.1.17)),

2)beta coronavirus (B.1.351),

3)gamma coronavirus (P.1), and

4)delta coronavirus (B.1.617.2)[2]

On 11th November 2021, a new variant was discovered in Botswana. Later many parts of South Africa reported this variant. World Health Organization (WHO), on 26th November 2021 classified this mutant as a variant of concern and named it as Omicron (B.1.1.529). The Omicron variant is the most heavily mutated variant among all the VOC so far, which paves the way for enhanced transmissibility and partial resistance to immunity induced by COVID-19 vaccines. Following the D614G, Beta/Gamma, and Delta VOCs, the SARS-CoV-2 Omicron variant could be the catalyst for the fourth wave of the COVID-19 outbreak to sweep the globe.[6]

To control COVID-19's super spread event and its impact on global health care infrastructure, the WHO has substantiated on early diagnosis, prevention, social distancing, proper sanitization, and complete lockdown-like strategies. Additionally, the guidelines approved by various national and international authorities about the do's and don'ts have been made available to national and international platforms. Apart from this, rigorous efforts being made by our researchers and medical practitioners to disseminate accurate details mimetic to etiology, pathogenesis, clinical course, and protective measures for the widespread COVID-19 disease across the communities, one of the fastest and reliable sources is real-time counts infected cases worldwide.[5]

EVOLUTION OF SARS-COV-2

Since the outbreak of COVID-19 disease in December 2019 in Wuhan, China, the interest of epidemiologists has piqued in assessing the rationale behind the eruption of SARS-CoV-2 in humans, including the involvement of animal reservoir, endemic circulation, co-infection, recombination events within RNA segments, and its time of divergence from animal species.

In December 2019, when the cases of pneumonia were epidemiologically related to the open-air seafood market in Wuhan, China, the local authorities in China provisioned an epidemiological alert and issued a complete lockdown for a couple of weeks. After rigorous research and clinical implications, in January 2020, the scientists at Wuhan obtained a complete genome sequence from the infected people and obtained around 80% sequence similarity with SARS-CoV, confirming pneumonia to be a SARS-induced condition. Initially, this novel human pathogen was placed in the Sarbecovirus subgenus of the Coronaviridae family, the family in which SARS falls. The virus is responsible for more than 8,200 cases from 2002–2003. Later, by mid-January 2020, the virus did super-spread within China, and by mid-March 2020 was labeled as pandemic status. This, in turn, enhanced the concern of the medical fraternity to prevent its spread and, at the same time, the researchers across the world were busy identifying the strain affecting millions of lives. With the subsequent studies and ongoing reports, the virus was named SARS-CoV-2 by the International Committee on Taxonomy of Viruses (ICTV) study group and also named hCoV-19 .[5]

For the first time in a consortium on virological.org led by Zhang on January 10, 2020 (GMT), the advent of the first genome sequence of SARS-CoV-2, Wuhan-Hu-1 assisted the researchers to understand the ancestry of this novel coronavirus (SARS-CoV-2). Later the data from the bioinformatics analysis has evidenced the homology between SARS-CoV-2 and other members of the coronavirus family, especially with the beta-coronavirus 2B. Thus further studies had been undertaken on SARS-CoV-2 by considering it to be a new member of beta-coronavirus 2B lineage infecting humans. Upon aligning the full-length genome sequence of SARS-CoV-2 and obtainable genomes of beta coronaviruses, scientists observed around 96% of sequence identity within the genomes of SARS-CoV-2 and SARS-like BatCov and RaTG13 coronaviruses. This indicates the bat origin of SARS-CoV-2 or, in other words, SARS-CoV-2 has been naturally evolved from bats.[5]

Concurrently, studies have also suggested Malayan pangolins to be the possible host in the emergence of SARS-CoV-2 infection in humans. Pangolins, the scaly ant-eaters belonging to the mammalian order Pholidota, are among the illegally trafficked mammalian species used for food and medicine purposes. Due to the extensive manhandling of these pangolins, researchers have decided to conduct a study on frozen tissue samples (blood, lungs, and intestine) obtained from 18 Malayan pangolins during an anti-smuggling task. In particular, data from high through put RNA sequencing has confirmed the Malayan pangolins to be the intermediate host of coronaviruses to humans, and later the readouts from sequence similarity search have demonstrated nearly 85.5–93% identity in the sequences of pangolin coronavirus genome and SARS-CoV-2. Hence, the local authorities in China have decided to remove pangolins from wet markets to avoid further zoonotic transmissions.[7]

VIROLOGY

Coronaviruses, a family of viruses within the nidoviruses superfamily, are further classified according to their genera, alpha-, beta-, gamma- and delta-coronaviruses (α-, β-, γ- and δ-). Among those, alpha and beta species are capable of contaminating only mammals, whereas the other two genera can infect birds and could also infect mammals.[8] Two of these genera belong to human coronaviruses (HCoVs): α-coronaviruses, which comprise human coronavirus 229E (hcov229E) and human coronavirus NL63 (hcovNL63), and β-coronaviruses, which are human coronavirus HKU1, human coronavirus OC43, MERS-COV (known as Middle East respiratory syndrome coronavirus) and SARS-CoV (referred to as severe acute respiratory syndrome coronavirus).[5] The severe acute respiratory syndrome CoV-2 (SARS-CoV-2) is now named novel COVID-19 (coronavirus disease 2019).[9] Genome sequencing and phylogenetic research revealed that the COVID-19- causing coronavirus is a beta-coronavirus that belongs to the same subtypes as SARS virus, but still exists in a variant group. The receptor-binding gene region appears to be very similar to that of the SARS-CoV and it is believed that the same receptor would be used for cell entry.[8]

Virion structure and its genome

Coronaviruses are structurally enveloped, belonging to the positive strand RNA viruses category that has the largest known genomes of RNA.[10] The structures of the coronavirus are more spherical in shape, but their structure has the potential to modify their morphology in response to environmental conditions, being pleomorphic.

The capsular membrane which represents the outer envelope usually has glycoprotein projection and covers the nucleus, comprising a matrix protein containing a positive-strand RNA. Since the structure possesses 5'-capped and 3'-polyadenylated ends, it remains identical to the cellular mRNAs.[11]

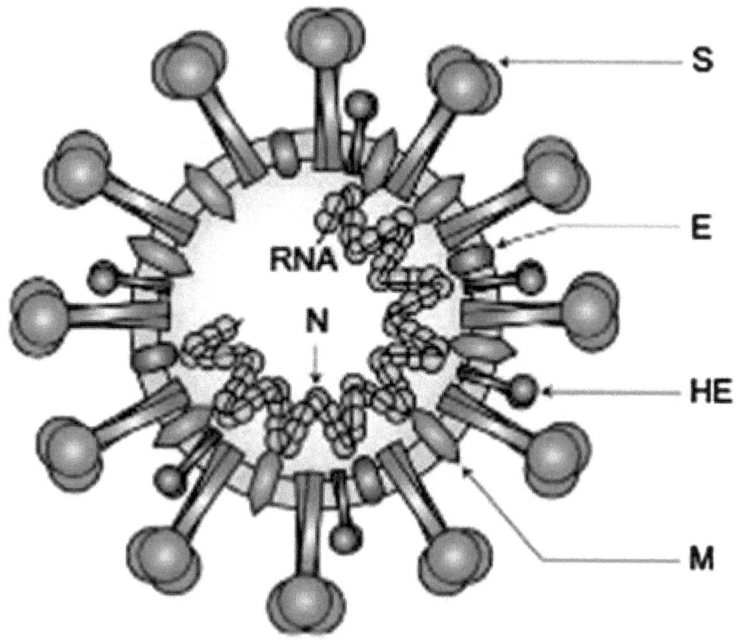

FIGURE 1 Virion structure and its genome

The structure is comprised of hemagglutinin esterase (HE) (present only in some beta-coronaviruses), spike (S), small membrane (E), membrane (M) and nucleocapsid (N), as shown (Figure 1).

The envelope containing glycoprotein is responsible for attachment to the host cell, which possesses the primary anti-genic epitopes mainly those recognized by neutralizing antibodies. The spike S-protein being in a spike form is subjected to a structural rearrangement process so that fusing the outer membrane of the virus with the host-cell membrane becomes easier. Recent SARS-CoV work has also shown that the membrane exopeptidase ACE enzyme (angiotensin-converting enzyme) functions as a COVID-19 receptor to enter the human cell.[8]

The genome of CoVs is a single-stranded positive-sense RNA (+ssRNA) (~30 kb) with 5′-cap structure and 3′-poly-A tail. The genomic RNA is used as template to directly translate polyprotein 1a/1ab (pp1a/pp1ab), which encodes non-structural proteins (nsps) to form the replication-tran (RTC) in a double-membrane vesicles (DMVs). Subsequently, a nested set of sub genomic RNAs (sgRNAs) are synthesized by RTC in a manner of discontinuous transcription. These sub genomic messenger RNAs (mRNAs) possess common 5′-leader and 3′-terminal sequences. Transcription termination and subsequent acquisition of a leader RNA occurs at transcription regulatory

VIROLOGY

sequences, located between open reading frames (ORFs). These minus-strand sgRNAs serve as the templates for the production of sub-genomic mRNAs.[10]

The genome size of the SARS-CoV varies from 29.0 kb to 30.2 kb. Its genome structure follows the characteristic gene order of other known CoVs: the 5′ two thirds of the genome comprises ORF1ab encoding replicase polyproteins, while the 3′ one third consists of genes encoding structural proteins including S, envelope (E), membrane (M), and N proteins (Fig. 2). Both the 5′ and 3′ ends of the SARS-CoV genome contain short untranslated regions. The translational product of ORF1ab is cleaved by proteases encoded by SARS-CoV itself into 16 nsps, which include major enzymes such as papain-like protease(s) (PLpro), chymotrypsin-like protease (3CLpro), RNA-dependent RNA polymerase (RdRp) and helicase (Hel).[11]

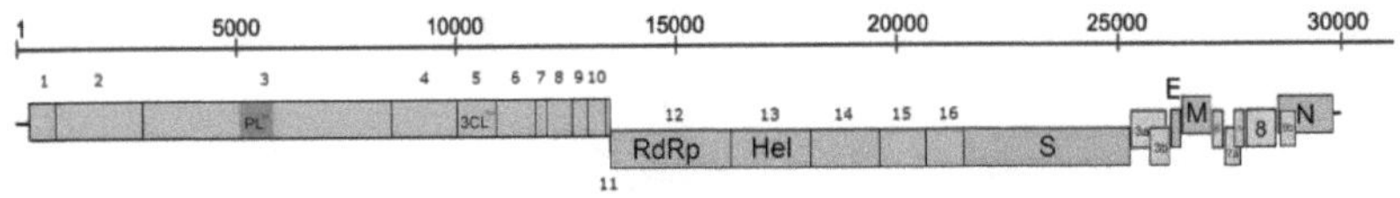

Fig. 2. Genome organization of SARS-CoV. ORF1ab with nsp1–16 are colored in blue. Structural proteins including S, E, M and N are in pink. Accessory proteins were numbered and in yellow.

Viral replication

Usually replication of coronavirus occurs within the cytoplasm and is closely associated with endoplasmic reticulum and other cellular membrane organelles. Human coronaviruses are thought to invade cells, primarily through different receptors. For 229E and OC43, amino peptidase-N (AP-N) and a sialic acid containing receptor, respectively, were known to function in this role. After the virus enters the host cell and uncoating process occurs, the genome is transcribed, and then, translated.[11] A characteristic feature of replication is that all mRNAs form an enclosed group of typical 3′ ends; only the special portions of the 5′ ends are translated. In total, about 7 mRNAs are produced. The shortest mRNA codes and the others can express the synthesis of another genome segment for nucleoprotein. At the cell membrane, these proteins are collected and genomic RNA is initiated as a mature particle type by burgeoning from internal cell membranes.[8]

PATHOPHYSIOLOGY

The Host Defense Against SARS-CoV-2

Early in infection, SARS-CoV-2 targets cells, such as nasal and bronchial epithelial cells and pneumocystis, through the viral structural spike (S) protein that binds to the angiotensin-converting enzyme 2 (ACE2) receptor7 (Figure 3). The type 2 transmembrane serine protease (TMPRSS2), present in the host cell, promotes viral uptake by cleaving ACE2 and activating the SARS-CoV-2 S protein, which mediates corona virus entry into host cells. ACE2 and TMPRSS2 are expressed in host target cells, particularly alveolar epithelial type II cells. Similar to other respiratory viral diseases, such as influenza, profound lymphopenia may occur in individuals with COVID-19 when SARS-CoV-2 infects and kills T lymphocyte cells. In addition, the viral inflammatory response, consisting of both the innate and the adaptive immune response (comprising humoral and cell-mediated immunity), impairs lymphopoiesis and increases lymphocyte apoptosis. AlthoughupregulationofACE2 receptors from ACE inhibitor and angiotensin receptor blocker medications has been hypothesized to increase susceptibility toSARS-CoV-2 infection.

later stages of infection, when viral replication accelerates, epithelial-endothelial barrier integrity is compromised. In addition to epithelial cells, SARS-CoV-2 infects pulmonary capillary endothelial cells, accentuating the inflammatory response and triggering an influx of monocytes and neutrophils. Autopsy studies have shown diffuse thickening of the alveolar wall with mononuclear cells and macrophages infiltrating airspaces in addition to endothelialitis. Interstitial mononuclear inflammatory infiltrates and edema develop and appear as ground-glass opacities on computed tomographic imaging. Pulmonary edema filling the alveolar spaces with hyaline membrane formation follows, compatible with early-phase acute respiratory distress syndrome (ARDS). Bradykinin-dependent lung angioedema may contribute to disease. Collectively, endothelial barrier disruption, dysfunctional alveolar-capillary oxygen transmission, and impaired oxygen diffusion capacity are characteristic features of COVID-19.

severe COVID-19, fulminant activation of coagulation and consumption of clotting factors occurs. Inflamed lung tissues and pulmonary endothelial cells may result in micro thrombi formation and contribute to the high incidence of thrombotic complications, such as deep venous thrombosis, pulmonary embolism, and thrombotic arterial complications (e.g., limb ischemia, ischemic stroke, myocardial infarction) in critically ill patients. The development of viral sepsis, defined as life threatening organ dysfunction caused by a dysregulated host response to infection, may further contribute to multi-organ failure.[13]

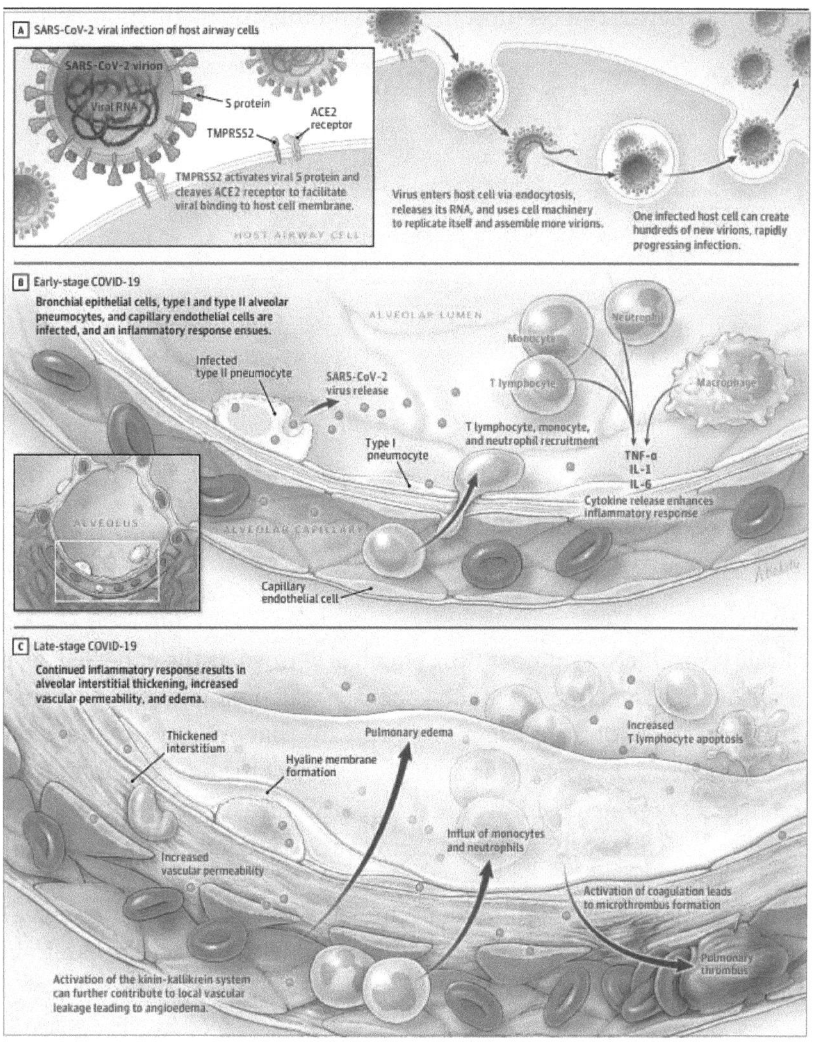

Figure 3 Immunopathogenesis Of Coronavirus Disease 2019

MODE OF TRANSMISSION

The primary mode of transmission of SARS-CoV-2 is via exposure to respiratory droplets carrying the infectious virus from close contact or droplet transmission from pre-symptomatic, asymptomatic, or symptomatic individuals harboring the virus.[2]

Droplet transmission occurs through direct contact when a person is exposed to infective respiratory droplets when they are within 1 m of someone with respiratory symptoms including coughing and sneezing. Being within this distance puts the individual at risk of having their mucous membranes, including their mouth, nose and eyes, exposed to the droplets . Transmission can also occur through indirect contact by way of fomites on surfaces in the immediate environment around the infected person.[8]

Airborne transmission may be possible when aerosol-generating procedures are performed including endotracheal intubation, cardiopulmonary resuscitation, administration of nebulized treatments, and others. Transmission of the virus can occur in the pre-symptomatic incubation period.

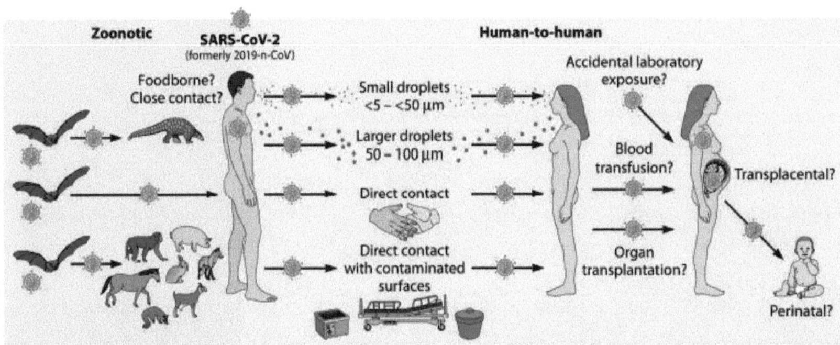

Figure 4- Potential transmission routes for SAR-COV-2

In terms of infectivity, the basic reproductive number (R0), which is defined as the expected average number of additional infectious cases that one infectious case can generate, was thought to range from 2.2 to 2.7 for SARS-CoV-2 infection in the early stages of the epidemic. This means that one person infected with SARS-CoV-2 can spread the infection to ~2.2–2.7 people. This number is subject to change with the progression of this pandemic, especially following the introduction of better control measures. The R0 for SARS-CoV was estimated to be around 3 after critically comparing various independent studies.[7]

There might be the point where zoonotic (animal-to-human) transmission occurred. Although SARS-CoV-2 is alleged to have originated from an animal host (zoonotic origin) with further human-to-human transmission.[13]

Additionally, other potential and expected routes would be associated with transmission, as in other respiratory viruses, by direct contact, such as shaking contaminated hands, or by direct contact with contaminated surfaces. Still, whether blood transfusion and organ transplantation, as well as trans placental and perinatal routes, are possible routes for SARS-CoV-2 transmission needs to be determined.[14]

Risk factors

Individuals of all ages are at risk of contracting this infection and severe disease. However, patients aged ≥60 years and patients with underlying medical comorbidities (obesity, cardiovascular disease, chronic kidney disease, diabetes, chronic lung disease, smoking, cancer, solid organ or hematopoietic stem cell transplant patients) have an increased risk of developing severe COVID-19 infection. The percentage of COVID-19 patients requiring hospitalization was six times higher in those with preexisting medical conditions than those without medical conditions (45.4% vs. 7.6%). The percentage of patients who succumbed to this illness was 12 times higher in those with preexisting medical conditions than those without medical conditions (19.5% vs. 1.6%). Data regarding the gender-based differences in COVID-19 suggests that male patients are at risk of developing severe illness and increased mortality due to COVID-19 compared to female patients.[2]

Fewer COVID-19 cases have been reported in children less than 15 years. The clinical features of infected pediatric patients vary, but most have had mild symptoms with no fever or pneumonia, and have a good prognosis. Another study found that although a child had radiological ground-glass lung opacities, the patient was asymptomatic. In summary, children might be less likely to be infected or, if infected, present milder manifestations than adults; therefore, it is possible that their parents will not seek out treatment leading to underestimates of COVID-19 incidence in this age group.[15]

CLINICAL MANIFESTATION

Clinical symptoms have been shown to occur most commonly between days 4 and 5 from exposure; however, studies have shown that the incubation period can last up to 14 days. The most common symptoms reported in the literature so far include fever, cough, fatigue and shortness of breath, which are similar to other viral infections including the seasonal flu. Patients with COVID-19 may have an extensive range of clinical manifestations. The clinical attributes of COVID-19 may vary from patient to patient ranging from asymptomatic to acute respiratory distress syndrome (ARDS). In general, the disease manifestations of nCoV-2 are dominated by a respiratory condition known as interstitial pneumonia.

A person infected with SARS-CoV-2 will initially experience fever, sore throat, dry cough, headache, fatigue, restlessness, myalgia, anosmia, and dysgeusia. Later it may progress to mild to moderate pneumonia followed by hypoxia, and if left undiagnosed and untreated, then it may further lead to severe complications such as acute respiratory disease syndrome (ARDS) and systemic inflammatory response syndrome (SIRS), and multi-organ failure (MOF) and/or shock. Regardless of respiratory symptoms, unrestricted SARS-CoV2 infection may stimulate a severe immune reaction called a "Cytokine storm," in which a body dissipates too many cytokines in the blood very quickly and uncontrollably.

As a result, the production of neutrophils, proinflammatory cytokines (IL-1b, IL-6, TNF-a, etc.), and chemokines (Ccl1, CXCl10, Ccl3, etc.) exceeds the levels of anti-inflammatory cytokines in the body, which in turn leads to multi-organ damages. The majority of patients together with the asymptomatic ones are reported to exhibit diffused bilateral pneumonia surrounded with ground-glassy opacity either progressing or co-existing with consolidation.[5]

Patients with SARS-CoV-2 infection can experience a range of clinical manifestations, from no symptoms to critical illness, given by CDC. In general, adults with SARS-CoV-2 infection can be grouped into the following severity of illness categories; however, the criteria for each category may overlap or vary across clinical guidelines and clinical trials, and a patient's clinical status may change over time.

- Asymptomatic or Pre-Symptomatic Infection: Individuals with positive SARS-CoV-2 test without any clinical symptoms consistent with COVID-19.

- Mild illness: Individuals who have any symptoms of COVID-19 such as fever, cough, sore throat, malaise, headache, muscle pain, nausea, vomiting, diarrhea, anosmia, or dysgeusia but without shortness of breath or abnormal chest imaging
- Moderate illness: Individuals who have clinical symptoms or radiologic evidence of lower respiratory tract disease and who have oxygen saturation (SpO2) ≥ 94% on room air
- Severe illness: Individuals who have (SpO2) ≤ 94% on room air; a ratio of partial pressure of arterial oxygen to fraction of inspired oxygen, (PaO2/FiO2) 30 breaths/min or lung infiltrates >50%.
- Critical illness: Individuals who have acute respiratory failure, septic shock, and/or multiple organ dysfunction. Patients with severe COVID-19 illness may become critically ill with the development of acute respiratory distress syndrome (ARDS) which tends to occur approximately one week after the onset of symptoms.[16]

ARDS is characterized by a severe new-onset respiratory failure or worsening of an already identified respiratory picture. The diagnosis requires a set of clinical and ventilator criteria such as chest imaging utilized includes chest radiograph, CT scan, or lung ultrasound demonstrating bilateral opacities (lung infiltrates > 50%), not fully explained by effusions, lobar, or lung collapse. If there are clinical and radiologic findings of pulmonary edema, heart failure, or other causes such as fluid overload, they should be excluded before assessing it to be ARDS. [15]

Although COVID-19, the illness caused by SARS-CoV-2, predominantly affects the respiratory system, COVID-19 can be considered a systemic viral illness given the multiple organ dysfunction associated with this illness.[2]

Oral manifestations:

Gustatory changes or taste impairments: Gustatory and olfactory changes can be the only symptom in mild cases of Covid-19 or the initial symptom in patients who ultimately present with more severe respiratory failure. The reported gustatory changes associated with Covid-19 are hypogeusia, dysgeusia and ageusia. The exact pathogenesis of SARS-CoV-2 and olfactory and gustatory dysfunction is not known. It is reported that angiotensin-converting enzyme 2 (ACE2) cell receptors are expressed in abundance on respiratory epithelium and oral mucosa especially tongue. SARS-CoV-2 has a great affinity for these receptors. Direct damage to nasal and oral epithelium and neuro-invasive nature of this virus can result in olfactory and gustatory disorders.[17]

In fact, it is often very difficult for the patient to delineate between taste and smell dysfunctions. There is a need to highlight Covid-19 cases presented with gustatory dysfunction (hypogeusia, dysgeusia and ageusia) in the absence of olfactory changes. Investigations such as whole mouth and spatial taste tests can be employed to identify the presence of gustatory dysfunctions along with localization of area of impairment and threshold sensitivity to a particular taste.[18]

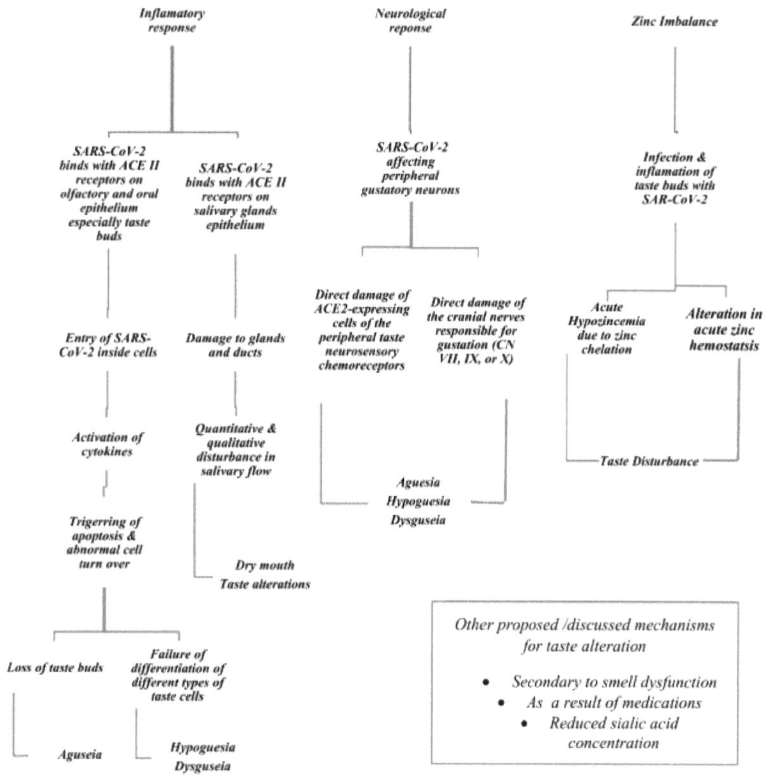

Figure 5 Proposed mechanisms for taste alteration in Covid-19. ACE2, angiotensin-converting enzyme 2; SARS-CoV-2, severe acute respiratory virus syndrome coronavirus 2.

Oral mucosal lesions- Many oral mucosal lesions are reported in Covid-19 confirmed and suspected individuals.[19] They include ulcers, erosions, blisters, plaque - like lesions, reactivation of herpes simplex virus 1(HSV1), and geographical tongue.[20] Oral mucosal lesions are presented along with common symptoms of Covid-19 or with other cutaneous manifestations.[21]

The lesions appear either before or along with systemic manifestations of Covid-19. Oral mucosal lesions Many oral mucosal lesions are reported in Covid-19 confirmed and suspected individuals. They include ulcers, erosions, blisters, plaque - like lesions, reactivation of herpes simplex virus 1(HSV1), and geographical tongue. Oral mucosal lesions are presented along with common symptoms of Covid-19 or with other cutaneous manifestations. The lesions appear either before or along with systemic manifestations of Covid-19.

It is stated in few publications that only oral symptom associated with Covid-19 is taste impairment and other oral lesions arise as a result of decreased immunity due to viral infection, opportunistic or secondary infection or treatment for Covid-19.[20]

Different possible mechanisms proposed for oral mucosal lesions are shown in Figure 6

Figure 6: Proposed mechanisms of oral mucosal lesion due to Covid-19. SARS-CoV-2, severe acute respiratory virus syndrome coronavirus 2;

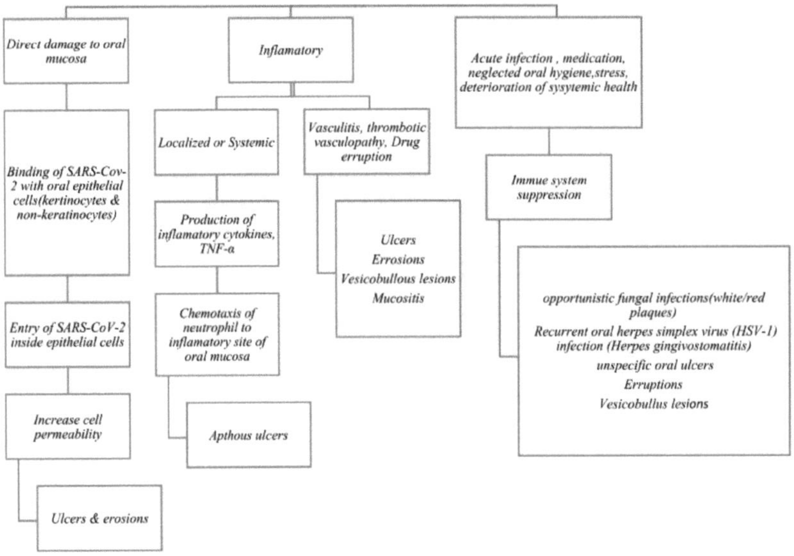

Ulcers & erosion: One of the most common oral complication associated with Covid-19 confirmed or suspected individuals is ulcerative lesions of the oral cavity.Tongue (dorsum and lateral boarder) is the most common reported site followed by hard palate and buccal mucosa. Irregular and painful ulcers either appear alone (single ulcers) or in the form of multiple tiny ulcers. Clusters of ulcers either resemble herpetiform ulcers or multiple apthoid ulcers with diffuse erythematous base. These multiple apthoid ulcer later on coalesce to form large ulcers with yellowish fibrin covering them, resembling erythema multiform -like disease. Ulcers, erosions and blood crust on labial mucosa along with palatal and gingival petechiae are also reported in one study.[19]

[18]Figure 7 (A) COVID-19 patient presenting a white plaque on the tongue dorsum, centrally located, associated with several small, circle-shaped yellowish ulcers resembling the late stage of herpetic recurrent oral lesions associated with candidiasis. A nodule located in the lower lip was observed, measuring approximately 1 cm in its largest diameter, suggesting a reactive lesion (fibroma).

(B) COVID-19 patient presenting atrophic areas surrounded by an elevated yellow-white halo classified as severe geographic tongue according to the severity index scoring system associated with fissured tongue. Also, the tongue's white lesions, suggestive of candidiasis, showed almost complete resolution.

(C) The patient, recovered from COVID-19, showing atrophic areas surrounded by an elevated yellow-white halo classified as moderate geographic tongue according to the severity index scoring system. We could observe a slightly erythematous area in the right palatine tonsil region; however, the patient reported being asymptomatic.

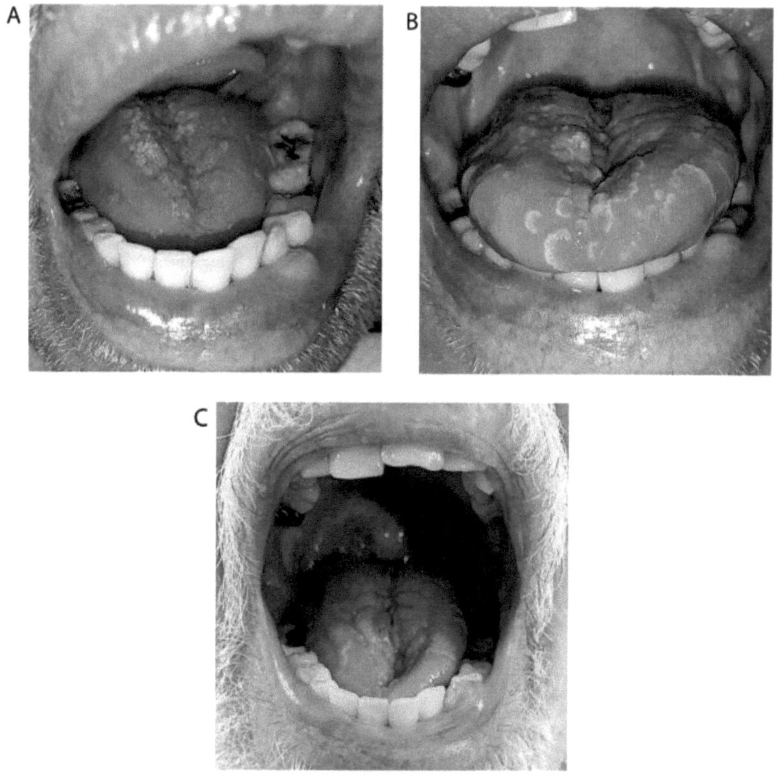

Figure 7

Plaques (white or red)- Candidal plaque -like lesions are also observed in association with Covid-19. Both red and white plaques were observed. They are located on the dorsum of the tongue and palate. They were also observed along with multiple tiny ulcers, taste changes, tongue and masticatory muscles pain.[18] Immune system suppression as a result of antibiotic therapy, deteriorating general health and neglected oral hygiene can be possible causes of these plaques.[19]

Vesicobullous lesions: Tongue and palate (soft and hard) are the most common reported location of these lesions.[20] These lesions mostly appear in association with cutaneous manifestations and show a range of presentation such as blisters, petechiae, erythematous lesions and erythema multiform -like lesions.[21] Erythema multiform -like lesions are most commonly reported lesions accompanied by skin target lesions.[22]

Figure 8- vesiculobullus lesions

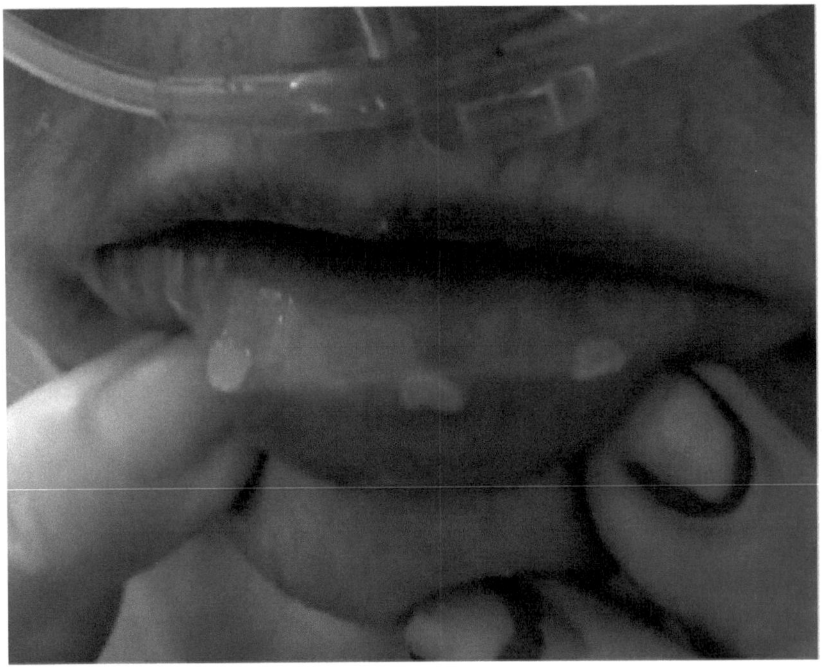

Figure 8

Figure 9 Clinical presentation of erythema multiforme (EM)-like exanthem in (a) Patient 1; (b) Patient 2; (d) Patient 3; and (e) Patient 4 showing coalescing erythemato-violaceous patches with a dusky centre, some of them with pseudovesicles in the middle, located on the back. Typical EM targetoid lesions were observed on (c) the buttocks of Patient 2 and (f) the thigh of Patient 4

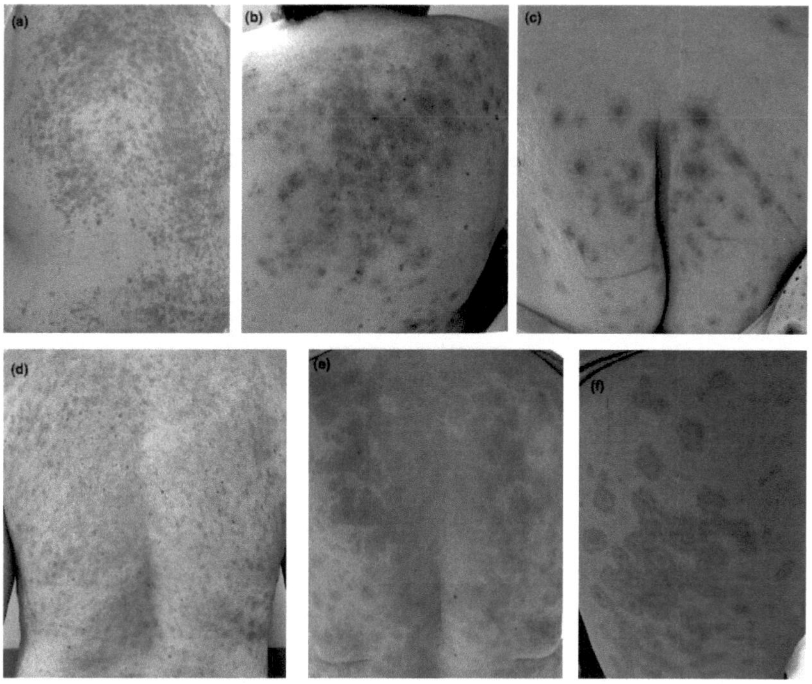

Figure 9

Gingival changes-Gingival changes such as generalized erythematous and edematous gingivae, gingivo-paradontal bleeding, necrotic interdental papillae and desquamative gingivitis are reported in the literature. They are reported in critically ill patients with neglected oral hygiene. In a Covid-19 suspected patient symptoms disappeared within 10 days of antibiotics and topical antiseptic mouthwash usage.[19]

Other manifestations Symptoms such as halitosis, tongue and masticatory muscle pain and swelling, geographical tongue, hyperplasia of papilla associated with taste changes and macroglossia are also reported along with fatigue and major symptoms of Covid-19 in few case reports.[19]

Cutaneous manifestations: Acral lesions resembling pseudo chilblains were the most common cutaneous manifestations noted in patients with COVID-19 based on the results of a meta-analysis study. Other cutaneous manifestations described erythematous maculopapular rash, vesicular rashes, and urticarial rashes. Notably, the appearance of a specific type was rash appeared to be dependent on the patient's age. Other uncommon rashes described were vascular rashes resembling livedo or purpura, especially in elderly patients, and erythema multiforme-like eruptions, mostly in children.

Figure 10 COVID-19-associated cutaneous manifestations. (a) Urticarial rash. (b) Combination of confluent erythematous rash on the chest with petechial lesions on the abdomen and upper extremities. (c) Acral chilblain-like lesions on the foot. (d) Vesicular exanthem. (e) Palpable purpura on the knees. (f) Livedo racemosa-like lesions on the thighs. All of the photographs belong to the authors' own collection.

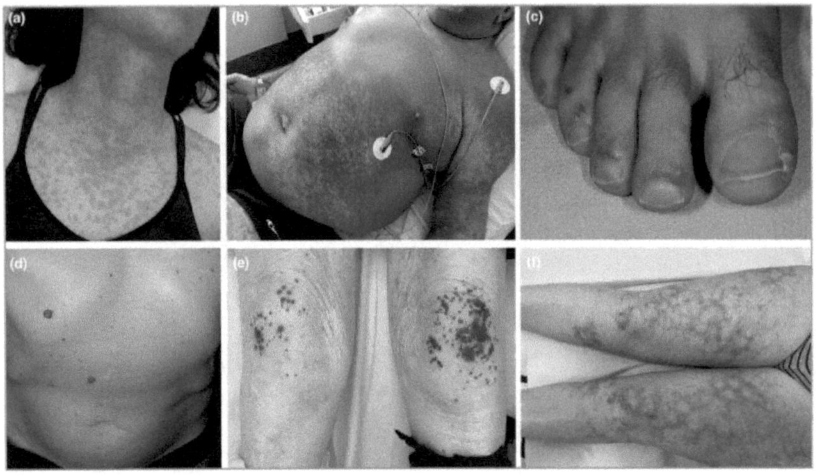

Figure 10

- **Renal manifestations**: Patients hospitalized with severe COVID-19 are at risk for developing kidney injury, most commonly manifesting as acute kidney injury (AKI), which is likely multifactorial in the setting of hypervolemia, drug injury, vascular injury, and drug-related injury, and possibly direct cytotoxicity of the virus itself. AKI is the most frequently encountered extra-pulmonary manifestation of COVID-19 and is associated with an increased risk of mortality.[23] Other clinical and laboratory manifestations include proteinuria, hematuria, electrolyte abnormalities such as hyperkalemia, hyponatremia, acid-base balance disturbance such as metabolic acidosis.[24]
- **Cardiac manifestations:** Myocardial injury manifesting as myocardial ischemia/infarction (MI) and myocarditis are well-recognized cardiac manifestations in patients with COVID-19. Other common cardiac manifestations include ACS, arrhythmias, cardiomyopathy, and cardiogenic shock.[25]
- **Hematologic manifestations**: Lymphopenia is a common laboratory abnormality in the vast majority of patients with COVID-19. Other laboratory abnormalities include thrombocytopenia, leukopenia, elevated ESR levels, C-reactive protein (CRP) lactate dehydrogenase (LDH), and leukocytosis. COVID-19 is associated with markedly elevated Ddimer, fibrinogen levels, prolonged prothrombin time (PT), and partial thromboplastin time(aPTT) in patients at risk of developing arterial and venous thrombosis.[26]
- **Gastrointestinal manifestations:** GI symptoms such as diarrhea, nausea and/or vomiting, anorexia, and abdominal pain are seen. The studies also reported that the mortality rate among patients with GI symptoms similar to overall mortality rate.[27]
- **Hepatobiliary manifestations:** Elevation in liver function tests manifesting as an acute increase in aspartate transaminase(AST) and alanine transaminase(ALT) are frequently seen in patients with COVID-19 infection. Hepatic dysfunction occurs more frequently in patients with severe COVID-19 illness.[28]
- **Endocrinologic manifestations**: Patients with underlying endocrinologic disorders such as diabetes mellitus who contract this virus are at increased risk of developing severe illness. Clinical manifestations such as abnormal blood glucose levels, euglycemic ketosis, and diabetic ketoacidosis have been noted in patients hospitalized with COVID-19.[24]
- **Neurologic manifestations:** Besides anosmia and ageusia, other neurological findings include headache,

stroke, impairment of consciousness, seizure disorder, and toxic metabolic encephalopathy.[29]

DIAGNOSIS OF SARS-COV-2:

- **The Real Time Reverse Transcriptase Polymerase Chain (rRt-PCR):**

The standard diagnostic mode of testing is testing a nasopharyngeal swab for SARS-CoV-2 nucleic acid using a real-time PCR assay. RNA tests can confirm the diagnosis of SARS-CoV-2 (COVID-19) cases with real-time RT-PCR or next-generation sequencing.[29]

At present, nucleic acid detection techniques, like RT-PCR, are considered an effective method for confirming the diagnosis in clinical cases of COVID-19. Commercial RT-PCR assays have been validated by the US Food and Drug Administration (FDA) with emergency use authorizations (EUAs) for the qualitative detection of nucleic acid from SARS-CoV-2 from specimens obtained from nasopharyngeal swabs as well as other sites such as oropharyngeal, anterior/mid-turbinate nasal swabs, nasopharyngeal aspirates, Broncho alveolar lavage (BAL) and saliva, shown in figure 11.

Figure 11: Collection of Nasopharyngeal swab for SARS-CoV-2 nucleic acid using a real-time RT-PCR

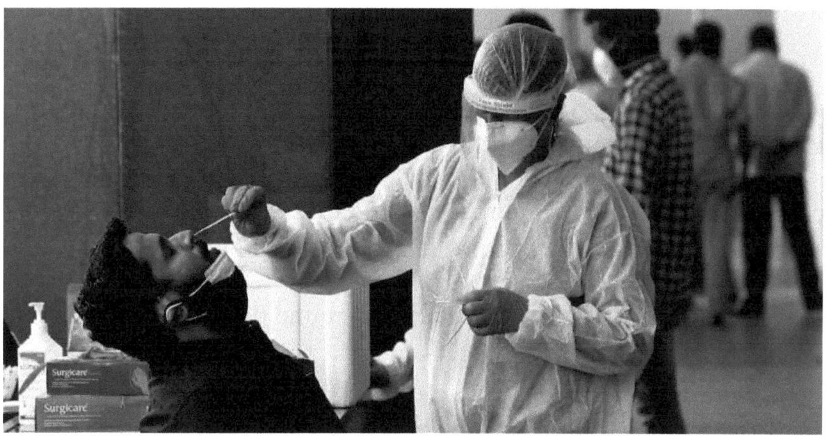

For specimen collection, with regard to upper respiratory specimens, nasopharyngeal and oropharyngeal swab should be considered, and for lower respiratory specimens, sputum and endotracheal aspirate or Broncho alveolar lavage should be considered. The collection of BAL samples should only be performed in mechanically ventilated patients as lower respiratory tract samples seem to remain positive for a more extended period.[2] Additionally, blood and stool specimen could be collected for clinical inspection. The study reported that the highest rates of positive were found from Broncho alveolar lavage fluid (93%), followed by sputum (72%), nasal swab (63%), fibro bronchoscope brush biopsy (46%), pharyngeal swabs (32%), feces (29%), and blood (1%).[30]

Several companies across the world are currently focusing on developing and marketing SARS-CoV-2-specific nucleic acid detection kits. Multiple laboratories are also developing their own in-house RT-PCR.[13]Food and Drug Administration (FDA) had granted 22 in vitro diagnostics Emergency Use Authorizations (EUAs), including for the RT-PCR diagnostic panel for the universal detection of SARS-like betacoronaviruses and specific detection of SARS-CoV-2, developed by the U.S. CDC (Table 1).[31]

Table1: Diagnostics available for SAR-CoV-2

TABLE 1 FDA-approved *in vitro* Emergency Use Authorization diagnostics available for SARS-CoV-2 as of 30 March 2020[a]

Developer	Diagnostic platform
Centers for Disease Control and Prevention (CDC)	CDC 2019-nCoV real-time RT-PCR diagnostic panel
Wadsworth Center, New York State Department of Public Health (CDC)	New York SARS-CoV-2 real-time reverse transcriptase (RT)-PCR diagnostic panel
Roche Molecular Systems, Inc. (RMS)	cobas SARS-CoV-2
Thermo Fisher Scientific, Inc.	TaqPath COVID-19 combo kit
Laboratory Corporation of America (LabCorp)	COVID-19 RT-PCR test
Hologic, Inc.	Panther fusion SARS-CoV-2
Quest Diagnostics Infectious Disease, Inc.	Quest SARS-CoV-2 rRT-PCR
Quidel Corporation	Lyra SARS-CoV-2 assay
Abbott Molecular	Abbott RealTime SARS-CoV-2 assay
GenMark Diagnostics, Inc.	ePlex SARS-CoV-2 test
DiaSorin Molecular, LLC	Simplexa COVID-19 direct assay
Cepheid	Xpert Xpress SARS-CoV-2 test
Primerdesign, Ltd.	COVID-19 Genesig real-time PCR assay
Mesa Biotech, Inc.	Accula SARS-Cov-2 test
BioFire Defense, LLC	BioFire COVID-19 test
PerkinElmer, Inc.	PerkinElmer new coronavirus nucleic acid detection kit
Avellino Lab USA, Inc.	AvellinoCoV2 test
BGI Genomics, Co. Ltd.	Real-time fluorescent RT-PCR kit for detecting SARS-2019-nCoV
Luminex Molecular Diagnostics, Inc.	NxTAG CoV extended panel assay
Abbott Diagnostics Scarborough, Inc.	ID Now COVID-19
Qiagen GmbH	QIAstat-Dx respiratory SARS-CoV-2 panel
NeuMoDx Molecular, Inc.	NeuMoDx SARS-CoV-2 assay

The sensitivity of PCR testing is dependent on multiple factors that include the adequacy of the specimen, technical specimen collection, time from exposure, and specimen source.[32]

However, the specificity of most commercial FDA-approved SARS-CoV-2 PCR assays is nearly 100%, provided that there is no cross-contamination during specimen processing.

SARS-CoV-2 antigen tests are less sensitive but have a faster turnaround time compared to molecular PCR testing.

- **Immunological Test:**

Rapid Tests Targeting Viral Proteins

In addition, rapid test design for the detection of viral protein is also in progress. i.e. viral nucleocapsid (N) and spike (S) are the main immunogenic proteins. While nucleocapsid protein is the most abundant and 90% similar to SARS-CoV, viral spike (S) protein is divergent and elicits strong immune response. However, the S1 subunit of spike protein was found to be specific for SARS-CoV-2, but the S2 subunit of spike protein was conserved across coronaviruses. Since many people have antibodies to the four endemic human coronaviruses, targeting specific part of the spike protein could avoid cross-reactivity. Currently, virus culture for detection is not recommend as it is time-consuming and requires biosafety.[30] Table 2 shows diagnostic options for covid-19.

Table 2: A comparison of diagnostic options for COVID-19.

Platform	Specimen/material	Type	Time	Sensitivity (%)	Specificity (%)	Cross-reactivity
NAAT	Nasopharyngeal swab; sputum; bronchoalveolar lavage fluid; blood	RT-PCR	240 mins	71–98	95	No
		CRISPR	40 mins	97	100	No
Serological	Nasopharyngeal swab; blood	Antibody	15–30 mins	92–100	93–100	Yes
		Antigen	15–30 mins	66–92	100	Yes
Imaging	Chest X-ray	Radiologist	15–30 mins	74.6	93.8	NA
	Chest CT-scan	AI	<5 mins	84.3	82.8	NA

Serology Testing: An antibody test can evaluate for the presence of antibodies that occurs as a result of infection. Antibody tests play an important role in broad-based surveillance of COVID-19, and many commercial manufactured antibody testing kits are available to evaluate the presence of antibodies against SARS-CoV-2 are available, shown in figure 12 .[2] There are important considerations for antibody testing, (i) timing of the test, (ii) previous infection, (iii) immune status of the individual, and (iv) cross-reaction, which can alter the test result.

However, a few antibody-based tests got emergency approval by the FDA, for instance, COVID-19 ELISA IgG Antibody Test from Cellex, which has a sensitivity of 93%, and qSARS-CoV-2 IgG/IgM Rapid Test from Mount Sinai Laboratory with 92.5% sensitivity.[30] Despite the numerous antibody tests designed to date, serologic testing has limitations in specificity and sensitivity, and results from different tests vary. However, an antibody test with a specificity higher than 99% and a sensitivity of 96% has been developed by the CDC, which can identify past SARS-CoV-2 infection. Antibody testing may be instrumental in broad-based surveillance of COVID-19 and evaluate the immunity conferred from infection or vaccination.[2]

Figure 12: Rapid Antigen testing kit

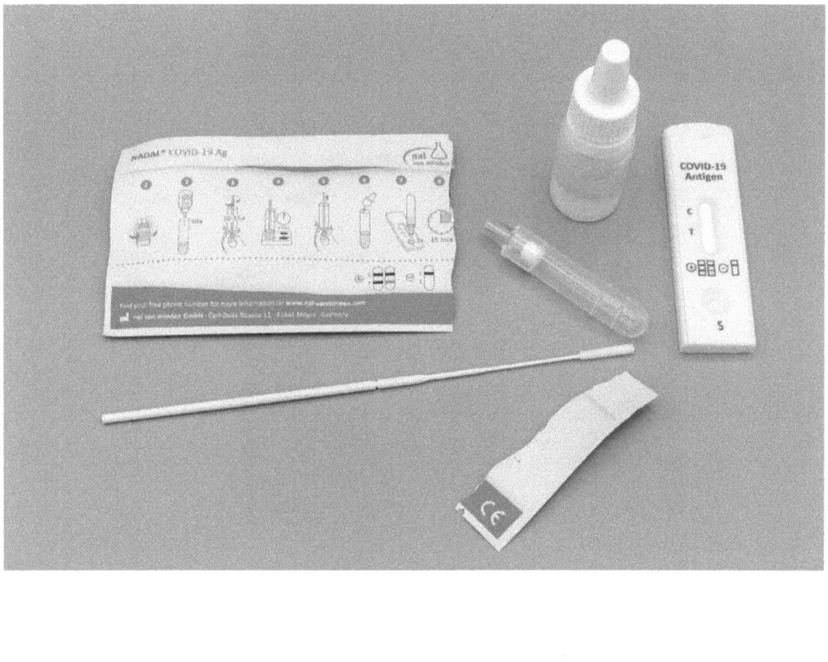

CRISPR gene editing tool has been employed to construct an accurate, faster, and simple-to-use SARS-CoV-2 detection test. DNA Endonuclease-Targeted CRISPR Trans Reporter (DETECTR) assay is based on CRISPR–Cas12 and it can distinguish SARS-CoV-2 with no cross-reactivity for related coronavirus strains using N gene gRNA within 40 minutes.

The result is visualized by using a FAM-biotin reporter molecule and lateral flow strips to capture labeled nucleic acids. Another CRISPR-based POC diagnostic is the SHERLOCK COVID-19 that incorporates a thermostable Cas12b enzyme from Alicyclobacillus acidiphilus. The test recently got FDA approval under emergency use authorizations.[33]

The test can be conducted by extracting RNA from patient samples and can be read out in less than an hour using a dipstick, without requiring extensive instrumentation. In India, a different approach was taken to build a CRISPR-based tool. The FnCas9 Editor Linked Uniform Detection Assay (FELUDA) used a highly accurate enzymatic readout for detecting nucleotide sequences. The assay is quick to provide output and can be used in rapid diagnosis.[30]

- **Imaging.**

Apart from detecting the presence of the virus, chest CT scan can demonstrate the disease status and severity. A recent study suggested that CT scan is more sensitive than the PCR procedure.[34] During the early stage of pneumonia, there are multiple small patchy shadows seen with interstitial changes, which is unusual in the lung periphery. Some cases could develop bilateral multiple ground-glass opacity, infiltrating shadows, and pulmonary consolidation with infrequent pleural effusion.[35]

However, CT scans has drawbacks as the mechanism cannot differentiate pneumonia and other pulmonary anomalies from COVID-19.[30]

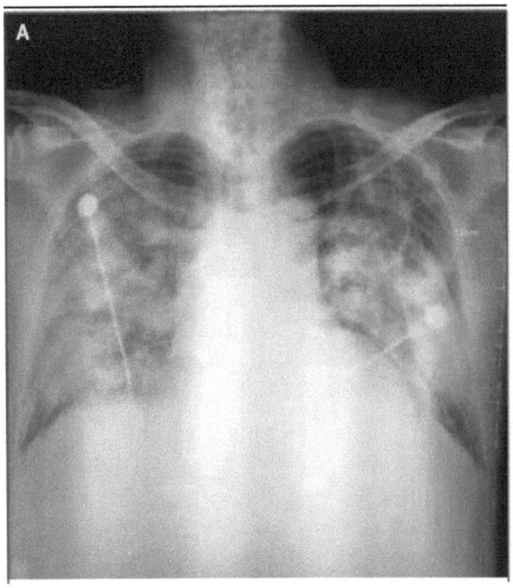

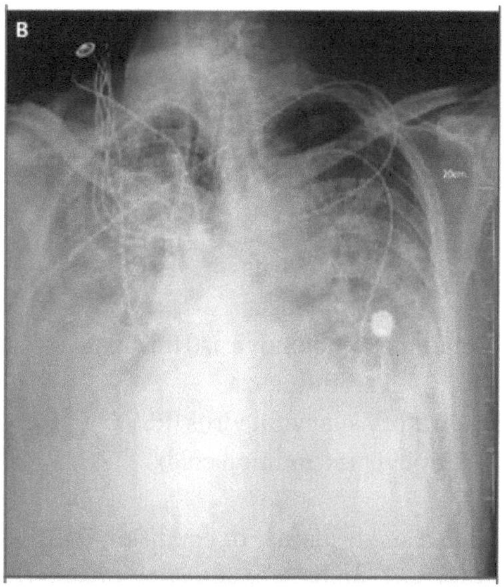

Figure 13: Shown are chest radiographs from Patient 2 on days 8 and 11 after the onset of illness. The trachea was intubated and mechanical ventilation instituted in the period between the acquisition of the two images. Bilateral fluffy opacities are present in both images but are increased in density, profusion, and confluence in the second image; these changes are most marked in the lower lung fields. Changes consistent with the accumulation of pleural liquid are also visible in the second image.[12]

Artificial Intelligence

Recently, artificial intelligence system based on deep convolutional neural network design was used to detect COVID-19 from chest radiography images. The tool provides quicker result and continues to get better with the addition of more data. Moreover, the machine learning approach shows potential to predict criticality in patients. Some AI inspired mobile application-based tools are in development to preliminary detect suspected COVID-19 patients.[36]

Other Laboratory Assessment-Complete blood count (CBC), a comprehensive metabolic panel (CMP) that includes testing for renal and liver function, and a coagulation panel should be performed in all hospitalized patients. Additional tests such as testing for inflammatory markers such as ESR, C-reactive protein (CRP), ferritin, lactate dehydrogenase, D-dimer, and pro-calcitonin can be considered in hospitalized patients. However, their prognostic significance in COVID-19 is not clear.[2]

Laboratory findings

Among COVID-19 patients, common laboratory abnormalities include lymphopenia, prolonged prothrombin time, and elevated lactate dehydrogenase. ICU-admitted patients had more laboratory abnormalities compared with non-ICU patients. Some patients had elevated aspartate aminotransferase, creatine kinase, creatinine, and C-reactive protein. Most patients have shown normal serum procalcitonin levels. COVID-19 patients have high level of IL1β, IFN-γ, IP10, and MCP1. ICU-admitted patients tend to have higher concentration of granulocyte-colony stimulating factor (GCSF), IP10, MCP1A, MIP1A, and TNF-α.[15]

DIFFERENTIAL DIAGNOSIS

The symptoms of the early stages of the disease are nonspecific. Differential diagnosis should include the possibility of a wide range of infectious and non-infectious (e.g., vasculitis, dermatomyositis) respiratory disorders.

- Adenovirus
- Influenza
- Human metapneumovirus(HmPV)
- Parainfluenza
- Respiratory syncytial virus (RSV)
- Rhinovirus (common cold)[2]

Differential diagnosis is the process by which a single disease or condition is differentiated from those having similar clinical features. Patients with COVID-19 can have co-infection or superimposed infection by other viruses or bacteria simultaneously. Differential diagnosis is therefore important to differentiate SARS-CoV-2 induced infection from other viral or bacterial and mycoplasmal pneumonia. Since a plethora of clinical manifestations is observed in COVID-19, there is an increased chance for incorrect diagnosis. For instance, a COVID-19 patient in Thailand was found to present with fever and rash and was initially mistaken for dengue.[37]

In regions with high burden of disease, differential diagnosis based on current symptoms, medical and epidemiological history, and a set of physical examinations will help determine the proper etiology. In case of bacterial pneumonia, there is usually high fever and coughing with thick, blood-tinged mucus or yellowish-greenish sputum with pus. Mycoplasmal pneumonia can also occur in any season, so blood culture or serum antibody determination is helpful for differential diagnosis.[30]

THERAPEUTICS AND DRUGS

Unfortunately, up until this point, there has yet to be a vaccine or proven effective therapy against SARS-CoV-2 infection. While many trials, including much needed randomized controlled trials (RCTs), are currently underway, the mainstay of therapy remains supportive care. This ranges from symptomatic treatment to ventilator support for patients with ARDS depending on illness severity. This also includes recognizing and treating superimposed bacterial infections and/or sepsis early on. Many of the current clinical trials are investigating drugs that were previously used to treat SARS-CoV and MERS-CoV. These will be discussed further below.

CHLOROQUINE/HYDROXYCHLOROQUINE:

Chloroquine and hydroxychloroquine are widely used antimalarial drugs. Hydroxychloroquine is a chloroquine analog with less drug to drug interaction and a better safety profile. Both chloroquine and hydroxychloroquine are shown to inhibit the growth of SARS-CoV-2 in vitro and decrease viral replication in a concentration-dependent manner. Hydroxychloroquine was found to be more potent. It has been hypothesized that both chloroquine and hydroxychloroquine may inhibit SARS-CoV-2 replication. They may do this by changing the pH at the surface of the cell membrane thereby inhibiting fusion in addition to inhibiting nucleic acid replication, glycosylation, and viral assembly and release.[38]

Few study found that hydroxychloroquine did not prevent illness related to COVID-19 or confirmed infection when used as post exposure prophylaxis within this timeframe.[39]

On June 15, 2020, the U.S. Food and Drug Administration (FDA) revoked the emergency use authorization granted on March 28, 2020 for chloroquine phosphate and hydroxychloroquine sulfate in certain hospitalized COVID-19 patients. They cite the serious cardiac adverse events and other protentional serious side effects to outweigh the potential benefits of their use.[40]

AZITHROMYCIN:

Azithromycin is a macrolide antibiotic that has been widely used in patients with chronic pulmonary inflammatory disorders and/or community acquired pneumonia for its anti-inflammatory effect.[41] However, there is limited data suggesting the beneficial effect of azithromycin in combination with chloroquine/ hydroxychloroquine in the treatment of ARDS in patients with SARS-CoV-2 infection. Hydroxychloroquine and azithromycin can both lead to corrected QT (QTc) prolongation, which can lead to fatal arrythmias. Therefore, they should be

used with caution in patients with prolonged QTc and those with certain medical conditions such as hepatic or renal disease.[7]

REMDESIVIR

Remdesivir is a novel nucleotide analog that incorporates into nascent viral RNA chains and causes premature termination inhibiting viral replication. Remdesivir has been shown to be an effective antiviral agent against beta-coronaviruses such as SARS-CoV and SARS-MERS in mice, non-human primates and in vitro. Despite its promising results in vitro, in vivo in animal models, and in compassionate-use studies in humans, remdesivir is still not approved by the FDA for use as a standard of care therapy due to lack of established data on safety and efficacy in humans. The biopharmaceutical company Giliad has initiated two phase 3 clinical trials to evaluate the safety and efficacy of this drug in COVID-19 patients.[7]

LOPINAVIR-RITONAVIR

Lopinavir-ritonavir is a protease inhibitor combination that has been used against human immunodeficiency virus (HIV) infection. This drug was proven to have in vitro activity against SARS-CoV; however, it does not seem to have a clear benefit during the current outbreak.[42] The use of lopinavir–ritonavir treatment in patients with SARS-CoV-2 showed no benefit with administration of the drug compared to standard care alone, which comprised of antibiotics, vasopressors, renal replacement therapy, extracorporeal membrane oxygenation (ECMO) and/or supplemental oxygen/invasive ventilation if needed. Gastrointestinal adverse events were higher in the lopinavir– ritonavir group compared to those receiving standard-care alone; however, adverse events were higher in the standard-care group overall.[43]

FAVIPIRAVIR

Favipiravir is an RNA polymerase inhibitor that is used for the treatment of influenza in China. Favipiravir is able to block the replication of RNA viruses by blocking the RNA-dependent RNA polymerase (RdRp) enzyme. Therefore, favipiravir may have antiviral activity against SARS-CoV-2, which is also an RNA virus.[44]

IVERMECTIN

Ivermectin is an FDA-approved medication for the treatment of various parasites and has an established safety profile in humans. Ivermectin has been shown to inhibit in vitro replication of various positive single stranded RNA viruses such as dengue and west Nile. This drug has recently demonstrated in vitro activity against SARS-CoV-2 when a single dose was able to control viral replication within 24–48 h. It is hypothesized that this is likely through the inhibition of importin α/β1 heterodimer, which mediates nuclear import of viral proteins, a process that many RNA viruses rely on during infection. The FDA has not yet approved ivermectin for the prevention or treatment of SARS-CoV-2 infection.[45]

CORTICOSTEROIDS

The use of glucocorticoids in patients with SARS-CoV-2 infection, especially in those with severe disease, was a point of major controversy. The rationale behind their use is to decrease lung inflammation as seen in ARDS. However, this comes with adverse effects such as inhibiting the immune response and thus increasing the risk of secondary infections as well as delaying viral clearance. Dexamethasone for 10 days use reduced 28-days mortality among those with severe disease (i.e., those receiving invasive mechanical ventilation or oxygen support) but not among patients with mild disease (i.e., those who did not receive any respiratory support).[46]

CONVALESCENT PLASMA

Convalescent plasma (CP) therapy is a classic adaptive immunotherapy that has been used for decades in the prevention and treatment of various diseases. CP was used in prior epidemics including SARS-CoV, MERS-CoV, and H1N1 in 2009 and it showed successful results with a safe profile. Given the similarity between SARS-CoV-2, SARS-CoV, and MERS-CoV, CP may have potential efficacy in this current pandemic. Study says patients showed stabilization in their vital signs, decrease in inflammatory biomarkers (CRP, IL-6 and procalcitonin), and improvement of abnormalities on imaging.[47] In the United States, the FDA is accommodating emergent investigational application for the use of CP in patients with severe or immediate life-threatening SARS-CoV-2 infection, such as those in respiratory failure, septic shock and/or multiorgan failure.[48]

HEPARIN

As more studies emerge linking coagulopathies to COVID-19 including systemic thrombosis and DIC, this raises the question whether heparin should be used in hospitalized patients to prevent these complications. Study shows patients who received a prophylactic dose of heparin when they had sepsis-induced coagulopathy (SIC) score ≥ 6 and a d-dimer level >6-fold of upper limit of normal had decreased mortality. Based on the limited available data, the International Society of Thrombosis and Hemostasis (ISTH) recommends the measurement of d-dimer, PT, and platelet count for all patients with COVID-19 infection to help with risk stratification. The society also recommends the administration of low molecular weight heparin at prophylactic dose to all hospitalized patients with no contraindications.[49]

VITAMIN C

Vitamin C, also known as ascorbic acid, has antioxidant properties and plays a significant role in reducing inflammatory response. Studies have shown that ascorbic acid down-regulates the production of pro-inflammatory cytokines.[50] These concepts have generated interest in the use of ascorbic acid in the management of inflammatory conditions. Study says patients in the intensive care unit, intravenous infusion of high-dose ascorbic acid compared to placebo did not significantly reduce organ dysfunction scores or improve levels of biomarkers indicating inflammation among patients with sepsis and ARDS, two disease processes heavily associated with inflammation.[51]

ZINC

It has been shown that increased zinc concentration inside the cell can effectively impair replication of a number of RNA viruses such as influenza and polioviruses. A study showed that zinc in combination with zinc-ionophores like pyrithione inhibited the replication of SARS-CoV in cell cultures.[52] Therefore, zinc supplementation may be of potential benefit for prophylaxis and treatment of COVID-19 and it was currently under investigation in multiple clinical trials in combination with other agents including hydroxychloroquine, vitamin C, and vitamin D.[53]

MONTELUKAST

Montelukast has been shown to suppress oxidative stress and have anti-inflammatory effects. Use of high dose montelukast has been effective in the treatment of acute asthma. Because much of the morbidity and mortality from COVID-19 infection is due to excessive inflammatory processes, it is thought that montelukast may play a role in limiting the progression of disease. One of the protein complexes involved in cytokine production and inflammatory responses is NF-B (nuclear factor kappa-light chain-enhancer of activated B cells). Therefore, inhibition of the NF-B signalizing pathway has been investigated for potential therapeutic options in inflammatory diseases. Montelukast inhibits the signaling of NF-B and other proinflammatory mediators. Its use in COVID-19 infection was being studied in a large clinical trial, which is in phase 3, compared with placebo.[54]

POTENTIAL VACCINES

To date, there was no vaccine proven effective against SARS-CoV-2 infection. The COVID-19 vaccine research and development landscape includes 115 vaccine candidates globally as of April 8, 2020. 78 of these candidates are confirmed, 73 of which are at exploratory or preclinical stages. One of the more advanced candidates that has recently moved into clinical development in the United States involves a messenger RNA platform (mRNA-1273), which encodes for the viral S protein of SARS-CoV-2 .[55]

PREVENTIVE MEASURES

For Public

The COVID-19 virus is transmitted between people through close contact and droplets. Airborne transmission may occur during aerosol generating procedures and support treatments (e.g. tracheal intubation, non-invasive ventilation, tracheotomy, cardiopulmonary resuscitation, manual ventilation before intubation, bronchoscopy)[56]; thus, WHO recommends airborne precautions for these procedures. For all, the most effective preventive measures include:

- maintaining physical distance (a minimum of 1 metre) from other individuals;
- performing hand hygiene frequently with an alcohol-based hand rub if available and if your hands are not visibly dirty or with soap and water if hands are dirty;
- avoiding touching your eyes, nose, and mouth;
- practicing respiratory hygiene by coughing or sneezing into a bent elbow or tissue and then immediately disposing of the tissue;

- wearing a medical mask if you have respiratory symptoms and performing hand hygiene after disposing of the mask;
- routine cleaning and disinfection of environmental and other frequently touched surfaces.

In health care settings, the main infection prevention and control (IPC) strategies to prevent or limit COVID-19 transmission include the following:[57]

1. ensuring triage, early recognition, and source control (isolating suspected and confirmed COVID-19 patients);

2. applying standard precautions for all patients and including diligent hand hygiene;[58]

3. implementing empiric additional precautions (droplet and contact and, wherever applicable for aerosol-generating procedures and support treatments, airborne precautions) for suspected and confirmed cases of COVID-19;

4. implementing administrative controls;

5. using environmental and engineering controls.[59]

For Health care workers

Additional transmission-based precautions are required by health care workers to protect themselves and prevent transmission in the health care setting. Contact and droplets precautions should be implemented by health workers caring for patients with COVID-19 at all times. Airborne precautions should be applied for aerosol-generating procedures and support treatments. Although use of PPE is the most visible control used to prevent the spread of infection, it is only one of the IPC measures and should not be relied on as a primary prevention strategy. In the absence of effective administrative and engineering controls, PPE has limited benefit, as described in WHO's Infection prevention and control of epidemic- and pandemic-prone acute respiratory infections in health care. [60]

Personnel Protective Equipment

The protection of our frontline health workers is paramount and PPE, including medical masks, respirators, gloves, gowns, and eye protection, must be prioritized for health care workers and others caring for COVID-19 patients. In view of the global PPE shortage, strategies that can facilitate optimal PPE availability include minimizing the need for PPE in health care settings, ensuring rational and appropriate use of PPE, and coordinating PPE supply chain management mechanisms,[60] shown in figure 14

Figure 14: Strategies to optimize the availability of personal protective equipment (PPE)

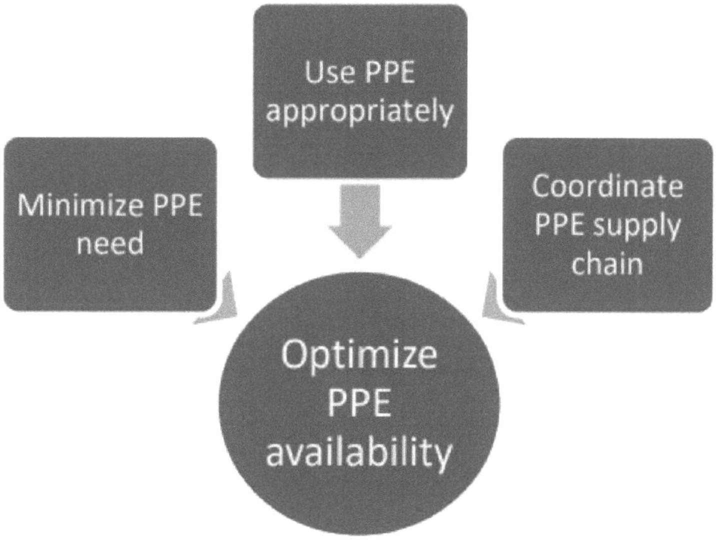

Table 3: Shows donning of PPE kit[61]

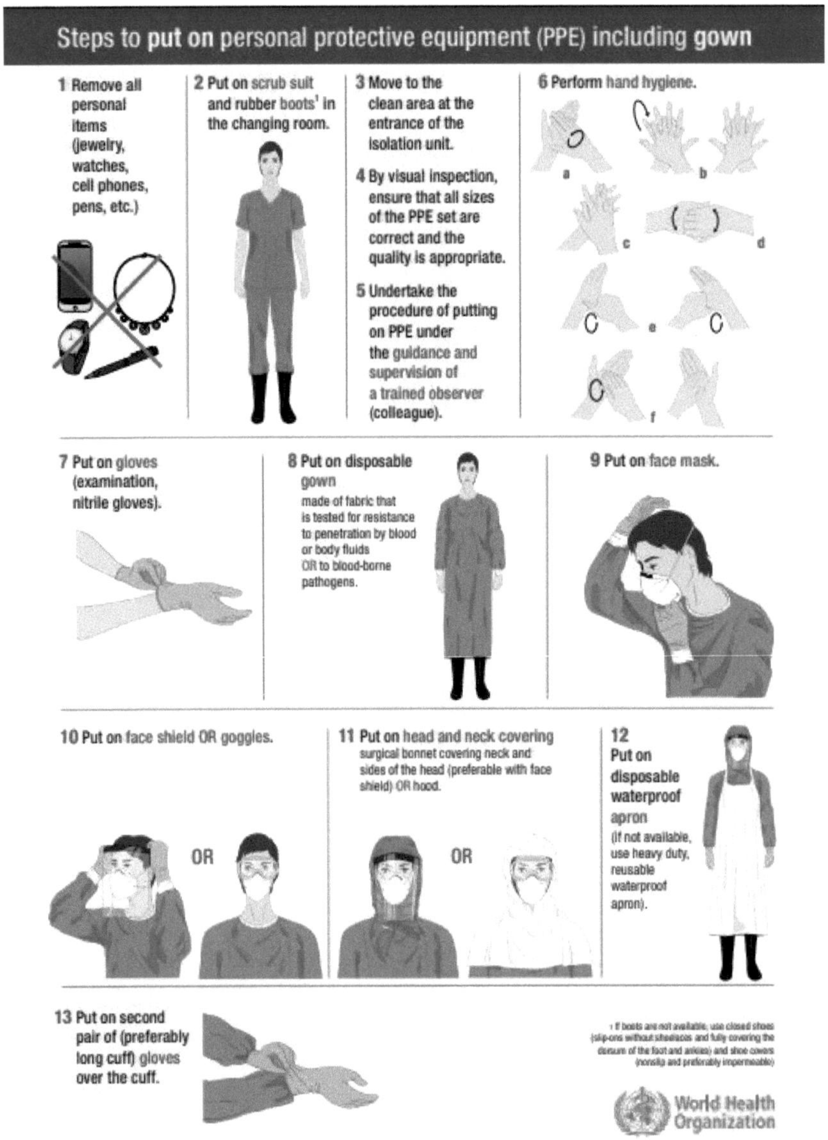

Table 3

Table 4: Doffing of PPE Kit

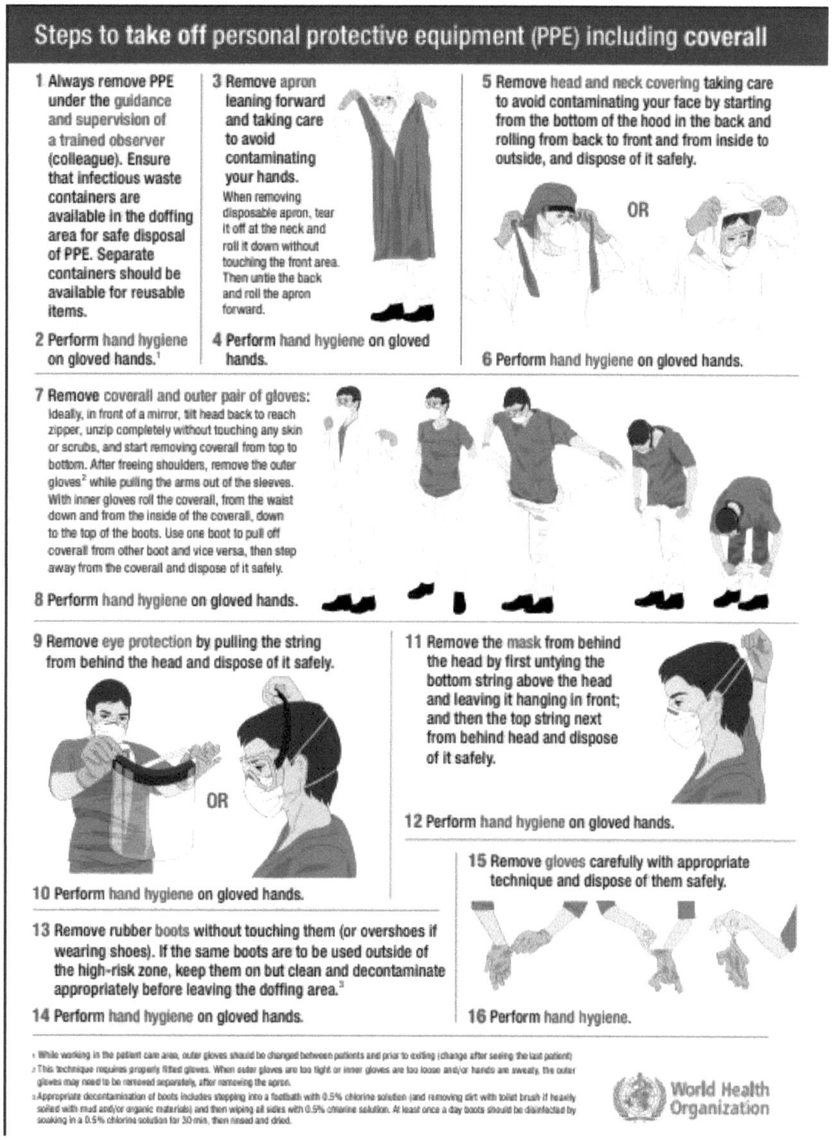

Table 4

Table 5: Recommended PPE during the outbreak of COVID-19 outbreak, according to the setting, personnel, and type of activity[60]

Setting	Target personnel or patients	Activity	Type of PPE or procedure
Health care facilities			
Inpatient facilities			
Screening[i] Clinical triage for prioritization of care according to severity (e.g. Manchester classification) should be performed in separate area for individuals with symptoms and signs	Health care workers	Preliminary screening not involving direct contact[c]	• Maintain physical distance of at least 1 metre. • Ideally, build glass/plastic screens to create a barrier between health care workers and patients • No PPE required. • When physical distance is not feasible and yet no patient contact, use mask and eye protection.
	Patients with symptoms suggestive of COVID-19	Any	• Maintain physical distance of at least 1 metre. • Provide medical mask if tolerated by patient. • Immediately move the patient to an isolation room or separate area away from others; if this is not feasible, ensure spatial distance of at least 1 metre from other patients. • Perform hand hygiene and have the patient perform hand hygiene
	Patients without symptoms suggestive of COVID-19	Any	• No PPE required • Perform hand hygiene and have the patient perform hand hygiene
Patient room/ward	Health care workers	Providing direct care to COVID-19 patients, in the absence of aerosol-generating procedures	• Medical mask • Gown • Gloves • Eye protection (goggles or face shield) • Perform hand hygiene
	Health care workers	Providing direct care to COVID-19 patients in settings where aerosol-generating procedures are frequently in place[ii]	• Respirator N95 or FFP2 or FFP3 standard, or equivalent. • Gown • Gloves • Eye protection • Apron • Perform hand hygiene
	Cleaners	Entering the room of COVID-19 patients	• Medical mask • Gown • Heavy-duty gloves • Eye protection (if risk of splash from organic material or chemicals is anticipated) • Closed work shoes • Perform hand hygiene
	Visitors[b]	Entering the room of a COVID-19 patient	• Maintain physical distance of at least 1 metre • Medical mask • Gown • Gloves • Perform hand hygiene

[i] The screening procedure refers to prompt identification of patients with signs and symptoms of COVID-19.

[ii] AGP: tracheal intubation, non-invasive ventilation, tracheotomy, cardiopulmonary resuscitation, manual ventilation before intubation, bronchoscopy.

Areas of transit where patients are not allowed (e.g. cafeteria, corridors)	All staff, including health care workers.	Any activity that does not involve contact with COVID-19 patients	• Maintain physical distance of at least 1 metre • No PPE required • Perform hand hygiene
Laboratory	Lab technician	Manipulation of respiratory samples Specimen handling for molecular testing would require BSL-2 or equivalent facilities. Handling and processing of specimens from cases with suspected or confirmed COVID-19 infection that are intended for additional laboratory tests, such as haematology or blood gas analysis, should apply standard precautions[9]	• Maintain physical distance of at least 1 metre • Medical mask • Eye protection • Gown • Gloves • Perform hand hygiene
Administrative areas	All staff, including health care workers.	Administrative tasks that do not involve contact with COVID-19 patients.	• Maintain physical distance of at least 1 metre • No PPE required • Perform hand hygiene

Outpatient facilities			
Screening/triage	Health care workers	Preliminary screening not involving direct contact[c]	• Maintain physical distance of at least 1 metre. • Ideally, build a glass/plastic screen to create a barrier between health care workers and patients • No PPE required • When physical distance is not feasible and yet no patient contact, use mask and eye protection. • Perform hand hygiene
	Patients with symptoms suggestive of COVID-19	Any	• Maintain spatial distance of at least 1 metre. • Provide medical mask if tolerated. • Perform hand hygiene
	Patients without symptoms suggestive of COVID-19	Any	• No PPE required • Perform hand hygiene
Waiting room	Patients with symptoms suggestive of COVID-19	Any	• Provide medical mask if tolerated. • Immediately move the patient to an isolation room or separate area away from others; if this is not feasible, ensure spatial distance of at least 1 metre from other patients. • Have the patient perform hand hygiene
	Patients without respiratory symptoms	Any	• No PPE required • Have the patient perform hand hygiene
Consultation room	Health care workers	Physical examination of patient with symptoms suggestive of COVID-19	• Medical mask • Gown • Gloves • Eye protection • Perform hand hygiene
	Health care workers	Physical examination of patients without symptoms suggestive of COVID-19	• PPE according to standard precautions and risk assessment. • Perform hand hygiene
	Patients with symptoms suggestive of COVID-19	Any	• Provide medical mask if tolerated. • Hand hygiene and respiratory etiquette

	Patients without symptoms suggestive of COVID-19	Any	• No PPE required • Have the patient perform hand hygiene
	Cleaners	After and between consultations with patients with respiratory symptoms.	• Medical mask • Gown • Heavy-duty gloves • Eye protection (if risk of splash from organic material or chemicals). • Closed work shoes • Perform hand hygiene
Administrative areas	All staff, including health care workers	Administrative tasks	• Maintain physical distance of at least 1 metre between staff • No PPE required • Perform hand hygiene
Home care			
Home	Patients with symptoms suggestive of COVID-19	Any	• Maintain physical distance of at least 1 metre. • Provide medical mask if tolerated, except when sleeping. • Hand and respiratory hygiene
	Caregiver	Entering the patient's room, but not providing direct care or assistance	• Maintain physical distance of at least 1 metre • Medical mask • Perform hand hygiene
	Caregiver	Providing direct care or when handling stool, urine, or waste from COVID-19 patient being cared for at home	• Gloves • Medical mask • Apron (if risk of splash is anticipated) • Perform hand hygiene
	Health care workers	Providing direct care or assistance to a COVID-19 patient at home	• Medical mask • Gown • Gloves • Eye protection
Points of entry at airports, ports and ground crossing as applicable			
Administrative areas	All staff	Any	• No PPE required
Screening area	Staff	First screening (temperature measurement) not involving direct contact[c]	• Maintain physical distance of at least 1 metre. • Ideally, build a glass/plastic screen to create a barrier between health care workers and patients • No PPE required • When physical distance is not feasible, yet no patient contact, use mask and eye protection. • Perform hand hygiene
	Staff	Second screening (i.e. interviewing passengers with fever for clinical symptoms suggestive of COVID-19 disease and travel history)	• Maintain physical distance of at least 1 metre. • Medical mask • Gloves • Perform hand hygiene
	Cleaners	Cleaning the area where passengers with fever are being screened	• Medical mask • Gown • Heavy duty gloves • Eye protection (if risk of splash from organic material or chemicals). • Boots or closed work shoes • Perform hand hygiene
Temporary isolation area	Staff	Entering the isolation area, but not providing direct assistance	• Maintain physical distance of at least 1 metre. • Medical mask

			• Gloves
	Staff, health care workers	Assisting or caring for passenger being transported to a health care facility as a suspected COVID -19 cases	• Medical mask • Gown • Gloves • Eye protection • Perform hand hygiene
	Cleaners	Cleaning isolation area	• Maintain physical distance of at least 1 metre. • Medical mask • Gown • Heavy duty gloves • Eye protection (if risk of splash from organic material or chemicals). • Closed work shoes • Perform hand hygiene
Ambulance or transfer vehicle	Health care workers	Transporting suspected COVID-19 patients to the referral health care facility	• Medical mask • Gowns • Gloves • Eye protection • Perform hand hygiene
	Driver	Involved only in driving the patient with suspected COVID-19 disease and the driver's compartment is separated from the COVID-19 patient	• Maintain physical distance of at least 1 metre. • No PPE required • Perform hand hygiene
		Assisting with loading or unloading patient with suspected COVID-19	• Medical mask • Gowns • Gloves • Eye protection • Perform hand hygiene
		No direct contact with patient with suspected COVID-19, but no separation between driver's and patient's compartments	• Medical mask • Perform hand hygiene
	Patient with suspected COVID-19.	Transport to the referral health care facility.	• Medical mask if tolerated • Have the patient perform hand hygiene
	Cleaners	Cleaning after and between transport of patients with suspected COVID-19 to the referral health care facility.	• Medical mask • Gown • Heavy duty gloves • Eye protection (if risk of splash from organic material or chemicals). • Boots or closed work shoes • Perform hand hygiene

Special considerations for rapid-response teams assisting with public health investigations[d]			
Anywhere	Rapid-response team investigators	Remote interview of suspected or confirmed COVID-19 patients or their contacts.	• No PPE if done remotely (e.g. by telephone or video conference). • Remote interview is the preferred method.
		In-person interview of suspected or confirmed COVID-19 patients or contacts without direct contact	• Medical mask • Maintain physical distance of at least 1 metre. • The interview should be conducted outside the house or outdoors, and confirmed or suspected COVID-19 patients should wear a medical mask if tolerated. • Perform hand hygiene

[a] In addition to using the appropriate PPE, frequent hand hygiene and respiratory etiquette should always be performed. PPE should be discarded in an appropriate waste container after use according to local guidance, and hand hygiene should be performed before putting on and after taking off PPE.

[b] the number of visitors should be restricted. If visitors must enter a COVID-19 patient's room, they should be provided with clear instructions about how to put on and remove PPE and about performing hand hygiene before putting on and after removing PPE; this should be supervised by a health care worker.

[c] This category includes the use of no-touch thermometers, thermal imaging cameras, and limited observation and questioning, all while maintaining a spatial distance of at least 1 m.

[d] All rapid-response team members must be trained in performing hand hygiene and how to put on and remove PPE to avoid -self-contamination.[60]

MANAGEMENT OF COVID-19[62]

ASYMPTOMATIC OR PRESYMPTOMATIC INFECTION

Individuals with a positive SARS-CoV-2 test without any clinical symptoms consistent with COVID-19 should be advised to isolate themselves and monitor clinical symptoms.[2]

MILD DISEASE

- Upper respiratory tract symptoms and/or fever WITHOUT shortness of breath or hypoxia
- Physical distancing, indoor mask use, strict hand hygiene
- Symptomatic management (hydration, anti-pyretics, antitussive)
- Stay in contact with treating physician
- Monitor temperature and oxygen saturation (by applying a SpO2 probe to fingers)

Seek immediate medical attention if:

- Difficulty in breathing or SpO_2 <93%
- High grade fever/severe cough, particularly if lasting for 5 days
- A low threshold to be kept for those with any of the high-risk features

MODERATE DISEASE

Anyone of:

1. Respiratory rate ≥ 24/min, breathlessness

2.SpO_2: 90% to ≤ 93% on room air

ADMIT IN WARD

Oxygen Support:

- Target SpO_2: 92-96% (88-92% in patients with COPD)
- Preferred devices for oxygenation: non-rebreathing face mask
- Awake proning encouraged in all patients requiring supplemental oxygen therapy (sequential position changes every 2hours)

Anti-inflammatory or immunomodulatory therapy:

- Inj. Methyl prednisolone 0.5to1 mg/kg in 2 divided doses (or an equivalent dose of dexamethasone) usually for a duration of 5 to 10 days
- Patients may be initiated or switched to oral route if stable and/or improving
- There is no evidence for benefit for injectable steroids in those NOT requiring oxygen supplementation, or on continuation after discharge
- Anti-inflammatory or immunomodulatory therapy (such as steroids) can have risk of secondary infection such as invasive mucormycosis when used too early, at higher dose or for longer than required

Anticoagulation:

- Conventional dose prophylactic unfractionated heparin or Low Molecular Weight Heparin (weight based e.g., enoxaparin 0.5mg/kgper day SC). There should be no contraindication or high risk of bleeding.

Monitoring:

- Clinical Monitoring: breathing rate, Hemodynamic instability, Change in oxygen requirement
- Serial CXR; HRCT chest to be done ONLY if there is worsening
- Lab monitoring: CRP, D-dimer, blood sugar 48 to 72hrly; CBC, KFT, LFT 24 to 48hrly

After clinical improvement, discharge as per revised discharge criteria

SEVERE DISEASE

Any one of:

1.Respiratory rate >30/min, breathlessness

2.$SpO_2 < 90\%$ on room air

Admit in HDU/ICU

- Respiratory support: Consider use of NIV (Helmetor facemask interface depending on availability) in patients with increasing oxygen requirement, if work of breathing is LOW
- Consider use of HFNC inpatients with increasing oxygen requirement
- Intubation should be prioritized in patients with high work of breathing /if NIV is not tolerated
- Use institutional protocol for ventilator management when required

Anti-inflammatory or immunomodulatory therapy:

- Inj Methylprednisolone 1 to 2 mg/kg IV in 2 divided doses (or an equivalent dose of dexamethasone) usually for a duration 5 to 10 days
- Anti-inflammatory or immunomodulatory therapy (such as steroids) can have risk of secondary infection such as invasive mucormycosis when used too early, at higher dose or for longer than required

Supportive measures:

- Maintain euvolemia (if available, use dynamic measures for assessing fluid responsiveness)
- If sepsis/septic shock: manage as per existing protocol and local antibiogram

Monitoring:

- Clinical Monitoring: work of breathing, Hemodynamic instability, Change in oxygen requirement
- Serial CXR; HRCT chest to be done ONLY if there is worsening
- Lab monitoring: CRP, D-dimer, blood sugar 48 to 72hrly; CBC, KFT, LFT 24 to 48 hrly.

After clinical improvement, discharge as per revised discharge criteria.[62]

Table 6: Clinical Management of Covid-19 Patients.

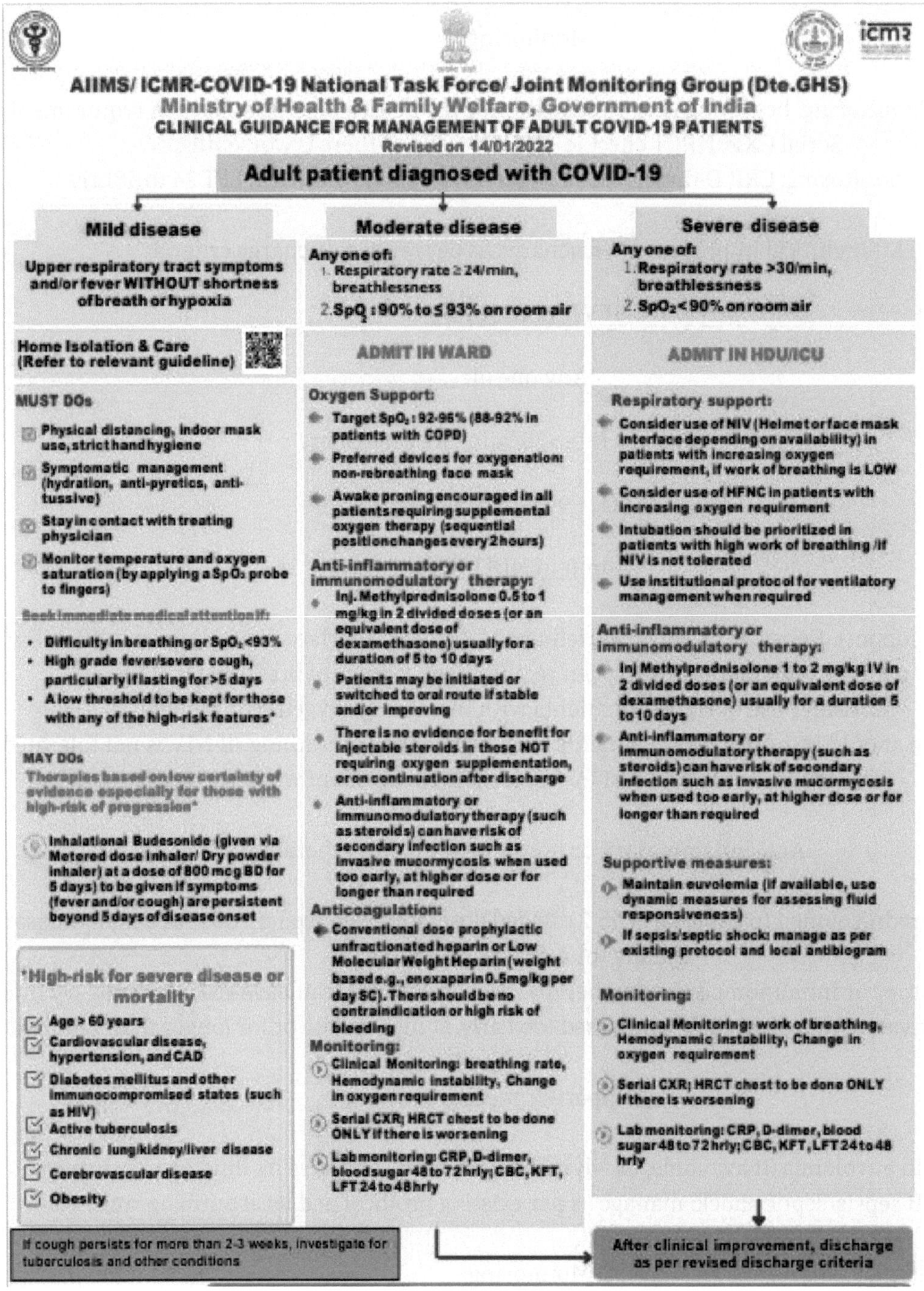
AIIMS/ ICMR-COVID-19 National Task Force/ Joint Monitoring Group (Dte.GHS)

Ministry of Health & Family Welfare, Government of India

CLINICAL GUIDANCE FOR MANAGEMENT OF ADULT COVID-19 PATIENTS

Revised on 14/01/2022

Adult patient diagnosed with COVID-19

Mild disease

Upper respiratory tract symptoms and/or fever WITHOUT shortness of breath or hypoxia

Home Isolation & Care (Refer to relevant guideline)

MUST DOs

- Physical distancing, indoor mask use, strict hand hygiene
- Symptomatic management (hydration, anti-pyretics, anti-tussive)
- Stay in contact with treating physician
- Monitor temperature and oxygen saturation (by applying a SpO_2 probe to fingers)

Seek immediate medical attention if:

- Difficulty in breathing or SpO_2 <93%
- High grade fever/severe cough, particularly if lasting for >5 days
- A low threshold to be kept for those with any of the high-risk features*

MAY DOs

Therapies based on low certainty of evidence especially for those with high-risk of progression*

- Inhalational Budesonide (given via Metered dose inhaler/ Dry powder inhaler) at a dose of 800 mcg BD for 5 days) to be given if symptoms (fever and/or cough) are persistent beyond 5 days of disease onset

*High-risk for severe disease or mortality

- Age > 60 years
- Cardiovascular disease, hypertension, and CAD
- Diabetes mellitus and other immunocompromised states (such as HIV)
- Active tuberculosis
- Chronic lung/kidney/liver disease
- Cerebrovascular disease
- Obesity

If cough persists for more than 2-3 weeks, investigate for tuberculosis and other conditions

Moderate disease

Any one of:

1. Respiratory rate ≥ 24/min, breathlessness
2. SpO_2 : 90% to ≤ 93% on room air

ADMIT IN WARD

Oxygen Support:

- Target SpO_2 : 92-96% (88-92% in patients with COPD)
- Preferred devices for oxygenation: non-rebreathing face mask
- Awake proning encouraged in all patients requiring supplemental oxygen therapy (sequential position changes every 2 hours)

Anti-inflammatory or immunomodulatory therapy:

- Inj. Methylprednisolone 0.5 to 1 mg/kg in 2 divided doses (or an equivalent dose of dexamethasone) usually for a duration of 5 to 10 days
- Patients may be initiated or switched to oral route if stable and/or improving
- There is no evidence for benefit for injectable steroids in those NOT requiring oxygen supplementation, or on continuation after discharge
- Anti-inflammatory or immunomodulatory therapy (such as steroids) can have risk of secondary infection such as invasive mucormycosis when used too early, at higher dose or for longer than required

Anticoagulation:

- Conventional dose prophylactic unfractionated heparin or Low Molecular Weight Heparin (weight based e.g., enoxaparin 0.5mg/kg per day SC). There should be no contraindication or high risk of bleeding

Monitoring:

- Clinical Monitoring: breathing rate, Hemodynamic instability, Change in oxygen requirement
- Serial CXR; HRCT chest to be done ONLY if there is worsening
- Lab monitoring: CRP, D-dimer, blood sugar 48 to 72 hrly; CBC, KFT, LFT 24 to 48 hrly

Severe disease

Any one of:

1. Respiratory rate >30/min, breathlessness
2. SpO_2 < 90% on room air

ADMIT IN HDU/ICU

Respiratory support:

- Consider use of NIV (Helmet or face mask interface depending on availability) in patients with increasing oxygen requirement, if work of breathing is LOW
- Consider use of HFNC in patients with increasing oxygen requirement
- Intubation should be prioritized in patients with high work of breathing /if NIV is not tolerated
- Use institutional protocol for ventilatory management when required

Anti-inflammatory or immunomodulatory therapy:

- Inj Methylprednisolone 1 to 2 mg/kg IV in 2 divided doses (or an equivalent dose of dexamethasone) usually for a duration 5 to 10 days
- Anti-inflammatory or immunomodulatory therapy (such as steroids) can have risk of secondary infection such as invasive mucormycosis when used too early, at higher dose or for longer than required

Supportive measures:

- Maintain euvolemia (if available, use dynamic measures for assessing fluid responsiveness)
- If sepsis/septic shock: manage as per existing protocol and local antibiogram

Monitoring:

- Clinical Monitoring: work of breathing, Hemodynamic instability, Change in oxygen requirement
- Serial CXR; HRCT chest to be done ONLY if there is worsening
- Lab monitoring: CRP, D-dimer, blood sugar 48 to 72 hrly; CBC, KFT, LFT 24 to 48 hrly

After clinical improvement, discharge as per revised discharge criteria

Table 6

Vaccines

There are several COVID-19 vaccines validated for use by WHO (given Emergency Use Listing). The first mass vaccination programme started in early December 2020 and the number of vaccination doses administered is updated on a daily basis.

The WHO Emergency Use Listing process determines whether a product can be recommended for use based on all the available data on safety and efficacy and on its suitability in low- and middle-income countries. Vaccines are assessed to ensure they meet acceptable standards of quality, safety and efficacy using clinical trial data, manufacturing and quality control processes. The assessment weighs the threat posed by the emergency as well as the benefit that would accrue from the use of the product against any potential risks.[63]

Table 7: As of 12 January 2022, the following vaccines have obtained EUL:

- The Pfizer/BioNTech Comirnaty vaccine,31 December 2020
- The SH/COVISHIELD and AstraZeneca/AZD1222 vaccine,16 February 2021
- The Janseen/Ad 2.S vaccine developed by Johnson & Johnson, 12 March 2021
- The Moderna COVID-19 vaccine (mRNA 1273), 30 April 2021
- The Sinopharm COVID-19 vaccine, 7 May 2021
- The Sinovac-CoronaVac vaccine, 1 June 2021
- The Bharat Biotech BBV152 COVAXIN vaccine,3 November 2021.
- The Covovax(NVX-CoV2373 vaccine,17 December 2021
- The Nuvaxovid(NVX-CoV2373) vaccine,20 December 2021

COVISHIELD and AstraZeneca/AZD1222 vaccines

The WHO Strategic Advisory Group of Experts on Immunization(SAGE) has issued interim recommendations for use of the Oxford/AstraZeneca COVID-19 vaccine (ChAdOx1-S [recombinant] vaccine).

Who can be vaccinated?

- The vaccine is safe and effective for all individuals aged 18 and above. In line with the WHO Prioritization Raodmap and the WHO Values Framework older adults, health workers and immunocompromised persons should be prioritised.
- The Astra-Zeneca vaccine can be offered to people who have had COVID-19 in the past. But individuals may choose to delay vaccination for 3 months following the infection.
- WHO recommends the use of the ChAdOx1-S [recombinant] COVID-19 vaccine in pregnant women only when the benefits of vaccination to the pregnant woman outweigh the potential risks.
- WHO does not recommend pregnancy testing prior to vaccination. WHO does not recommend delaying pregnancy or terminating pregnancy because of vaccination.
- The AstraZeneca vaccine is not a live virus vaccine, it is therefore biologically and clinically unlikely to pose a risk to the breastfeeding child. WHO does not recommend discontinuing breastfeeding because of vaccination.

Adverse effects

The Global Advisory Committee on Vaccine Safety, a group of experts that provides independent and authoritative guidance to the WHO on the topic of safe vaccine use, receives and assesses reports of suspected safety events of potentially international impact.

A very rare adverse event called Thrombosis with Thrombocytopenia Syndrome (TTS), involving unusual and severe blood clotting events associated with low platelet counts, has been reported after vaccination with this vaccine. In countries with ongoing SARS-CoV-2 transmission, the benefit of vaccination in protecting against COVID-19 far outweighs the risks.

Guillain-Barré syndrome (GBS) has been reported very rarely following vaccination. However, a causal relationship with the vaccine has neither been confirmed nor ruled out and more rigorous studies are needed to fully assess the significance of these events. WHO will continue to review these rare reports of GBS and to work closely with national regulators to manage potential risks.The AstraZeneca vaccine is safe and effective at protecting people from the extremely serious risks of COVID-19, including death, hospitalization and severe disease. 16 April 2021 statement of the WHO Global Advisory Committee on Vaccine Safety on AstraZeneca COVID-19 vaccine for reports of very rare side effects. The Council for International Organizations of Medical Sciences classifies rates of adverse events or medicines and vaccines as follows:

- Very common > 1/10
- Common (frequent) > 1/100 and < 1/10
- Uncommon (infrequent) >1/1000 and < 1/100
- Rare> 1/10000 and <1/1000
- Very rare < 1/10000

How efficacious is the vaccine?

The AstraZeneca vaccine has an efficacy of 72% against symptomatic SARS-CoV-2 infection, as shown by the primary analysis of data irrespective of interdose interval from trial participants who received 2 standard doses with an interval varying from about 4 to 12 weeks. Vaccine efficacy tended to be higher when the interval between doses was longer.

What is the recommended dosage?

The recommended dosage is two doses given intramuscularly (0.5ml each) with an interval of 8 to 12 weeks.

Is a booster dose recommended for this vaccine?

A booster dose may be considered 4 – 6 months after completion of the primary vaccination series, starting with the higher priority-use groups, in accordance with the WHO Prioritization Roadmap.[64]

The Bharat Biotech BBV152 COVAXIN vaccine against COVID-19:

On 3 November 2021, the Technical Advisory Group for Emergency Use Listing listed the Bharat Biotech BBV152 COVAXIN vaccine against COVID-19 for emergency use. The WHO Strategic Advisory Group of Experts on Immunization(SAGE) has issued interim policy recommendations for the use of the Bharat Biotech BBV152 COVAXIN vaccine.

Who can take this vaccine?

- The vaccine is safe and effective for all individuals aged 18 and above. In line with the WHO Prioritization Roadmap and the WHO Values Framework, older adults, health workers and immunocompromised persons should be prioritised.
- This vaccine can be offered to people who have had COVID-19 in the past. But individuals may choose to delay vaccination for 3 months following the infection.
- Given the adverse consequences of COVID-19 disease during pregnancy, WHO recommends the use of BBV152 in pregnant individuals when the benefits of vaccination to the pregnant person outweigh the potential risks. WHO does not recommend pregnancy testing prior to vaccination. WHO does not recommend delaying pregnancy or terminating pregnancy because of vaccination.
- WHO recommends the same use of BBV152 vaccine in breastfeeding and non-breastfeeding women. Data are not available on the potential benefits or possible risks of the BBV152 vaccine to breastfed children. However, as BBV152 vaccine is not a live virus vaccine, it is biologically and clinically unlikely to pose a risk to the breastfeeding child. WHO does not recommend discontinuing breastfeeding because of vaccination.

Who is the vaccine not recommended for?

- The vaccine is not recommended for people younger than 18 years of age. Safety and immunogenicity data for under-18s are currently being generated but until such data are available, vaccination of individuals in this age group is not recommended.
- Individuals with a history of anaphylaxis to any component of the vaccine should not take it.
- Persons with acute PCR-confirmed COVID-19 should not be vaccinated until after they have recovered from acute illness and the criteria for ending isolation have been met.
- Anyone with a body temperature over 38.5°C should postpone vaccination until they no longer have a fever.

Is it safe?

- SAGE has thoroughly assessed the data on safety and efficacy of the vaccine and has recommended its use for people aged 18 and above. The WHO EUL process also evaluates the quality of manufacturing along with safety and efficacy.
- Safety data is currently limited for persons above 60 years of age (due to the small number of participants of this age group in clinical trials). However, the trial data indicate that the vaccine has an acceptable safety profile for this age group and WHO recommends the vaccine for use in persons aged 60 years and over.
- BBV152 has been licensed for use in 23 countries globally; however, roll-out has been limited mostly to India where over 77 million doses have been distributed and used. Vaccine effectiveness studies are being conducted in India, and results will be available in the coming months.

How efficacious is the vaccine?

Vaccine efficacy against COVID-19 of any severity, 14 or more days post dose 2, was 78%. Vaccine efficacy against severe disease is 93%. In adults aged less than 60 years, efficacy was 79%; and in those aged 60 years and over it was 68%.

What is the recommended dosage?

- SAGE recommends the use of BBV152 vaccine as 2 doses (0.5 ml) given intramuscularly. The vaccine can be administered with an interval of 4 weeks. It is recommended that all vaccinated individuals receive two doses.
- If the second dose is inadvertently administered less than 4 weeks after the first, the dose does not need to be repeated. If administration of the second dose is delayed beyond 4 weeks, it should be given at the earliest possible opportunity.
- SAGE recommends that severe and moderately immunocompromised persons should be offered an additional dose of vaccine. This is due to the fact that this group is less likely to respond adequately to vaccination following a standard primary vaccination series and are at higher risk of severe COVID-19 disease.

Is a booster dose recommended for this vaccine?

- A booster dose may be offered 4-6 months after completing the primary series for the highest-risk groups, for example, older adults, health workers, persons with comorbidities.
- The benefits of booster doses are recognized following increasing evidence of waning vaccine effectiveness against mild and asymptomatic SARS-CoV-2 infection over time.[65]

POST COVID-19 COMPLICATIONS

The majority of COVID-19 patients recover within a week or two after infection; on the other hand, some of them have been noticed to experience moderate to severe post-COVID conditions. The data from COVID-19 hospitals from different nations suggest multiple health issues extending from a week to a month, even in people who did not have symptoms during COVID-19 infection. Predominantly it is the fatigue, muscle ache, headache, chest pain, cough, reduced performance, anxiety, lack of concentration, and depression like symptoms being experienced in the patients with the "Long COVID-19" condition. [66]

After diving deep into the health status of patients diagnosed with negative COVID-19, symptoms such as acute disseminated encephalomyelitis, Guillain-barre syndrome (GBS), acute necrotizing hemorrhagic encephalopathy (ANHE), acute neuropathy, etc. arising due to deregulated immune response, cranial involvement, and impaired central and peripheral nervous system are seen nowadays as a post-COVID condition and have become a matter of concern.[67]

Apart from these multiorgan effects, especially autoimmune conditions and multisystem inflammatory syndrome (MIS), i.e., a clinical condition in which edema occurs in different regions of the body due to elevated proinflammatory cytokines production have also been reported by the patients after a week of recovering from COVID-19.[68] Further progress in scientific and clinical investigations, pieces of evidence related to the post-COVID multiorgan condition with an extensive spectrum of manifestations of the disease, is brought into the knowledge. Examples of these multiorgan systems include rapid hair loss, feces with viral load for longer times, persistent palpitation, dyspnea, bone demineralization, uncontrolled diabetes, restrictive pulmonary physiology, elevated D-dimer, and COVID-19-associated nephropathy (COVAN) condition (a foremost pattern of renal injury in the majority of the African population).[69]

Our local health sectors and doctors are required to provide maximum attention to the COVID-19 patients who were on ventilators and hospitalized for longer durations as they are the ones who have consistently been reported to present the most complicated manifestations of the disease such as severe weakness, post-intensive care syndrome (PICS), post-traumatic stress disorder (PTSD), and the deadliest "mucormycosis" infection.[70]

MUCORMYCOSISis one of the devastating but rare fungal infections caused by exposure to a group of mucor moulds named mucormycetes. These mucormycetes, members of Mucorales order, are the cluster of fungi existing throughout the environment predominantly in soil rich in decaying organic matter such as animal drugs, composite piles, dead leaves, etc.[71] These fungi are more common in soil than in the air; similarly, they are noted to be more active in summers than winters or springs. Among these mucormycetes, it is the Rhizopus and Mucor species that are commonly known to cause mucormycosis.[72] As per the literature, the majority of us are encountered with microscopic fungal spores on a regular basis, as it is almost impossible to 100% circumvent the contact with mucormycetes. Although it is not really harmful to most people, for those with a weak immune system and recovering from some critical pathologies and still breathing in mucormycetes spores, then the possibility of infection in the sinuses, brain, lungs, and to other body parts may occur. This particular fungal infection is noted to be life-threatening in severely immunocompromised individuals or patients with diabetes mellitus.

Depending on its clinical features and anatomical localization, mucormycosis is broadly classified into six distinct classes:

(1) Rhinocerebral or rhino-orbitocerebral mucormycosis,

(2) pulmonary,

(3) cutaneous,

(4) gastrointestinal,

(5) disseminated, and

(6) uncommon presentations[73]

People infected with mucormycosis exhibit the presence of substantial angioinvasion followed by blood vessel thrombosis and tissue necrosis. As a result, penetration through endothelial cells lining blood vessels and their deterioration is observed commonly.[74] Based on a retrospective cohort study on the mucormycosis, involvement of some predisposition conditions has been noted; rhinocerebral, pulmonary, and disseminated mucormycosis are commonly known to affect those with uncontrolled diabetes mellitus (specifically in those with ketoacidosis), extensive burns, iron overload, solid malignancies, treatment with gluco-corticosteroids, or patients with neutropenia. GI mucormycosis may arise due to malnutrition.[75] However, cutaneous/ subcutaneous mucormycosis may affect the patients who underwent prolonged hospitalization and have been in touch with catheters and ventilators.[76]

The massive upsurge or according to local news "Tsunami of black fungus" has been observed in India in the wake of a spike in COVID-19 cases. Patients infected with this black fungus are presenting with nasal congestion, headache, and facial swelling. In the worst scenario, fever, cough, and dyspnea are also reported when the infection reaches the lungs.[77] Statisticians have claimed that steroids useful in curtailing the mortality rate in COVID-19 patients are potential factors for mucormycosis infection.[78] Other possible risk factors could be steam inhalation abuse, genetic pre-disposition, higher use of antibiotics, poor oral-nasal hygiene, repeated use of the same mask, etc.[79] However, experts are only left with either advising the use of Amphotericin B and posaconazole, or isavuconazole, or mostly the employment of surgical procedures to remove infected or dead tissue.[5]

CONCLUSION

Coronavirus disease (COVID-19) is an infectious disease caused by the SARS-CoV-2 virus.

Most people infected with the virus experienced mild to moderate respiratory illness and recover without requiring special treatment. However, some became seriously ill and require medical attention. Older people and those with underlying medical conditions like cardiovascular disease, diabetes, chronic respiratory disease, or cancer are more likely to develop serious illness. Anyone can get sick with COVID-19 and become seriously ill or die at any age.

The virus can spread from an infected person's mouth or nose in small liquid particles when they cough, sneeze, speak, sing or breathe. These particles range from larger respiratory droplets to smaller aerosols. It is important to practice respiratory etiquette, for example by coughing into a flexed elbow, and to stay home and self-isolate until you recover if you feel unwell.

The best way to prevent and slow down transmission is to be well informed about the disease and how the virus spreads. Protect yourself and others from infection by staying at least 1 metre apart from others, wearing a properly fitted mask, and washing your hands or using an alcohol-based rub frequently. Get vaccinated when it's your turn and follow local guidance.

Vaccine supply has improved, but absorption has not kept pace. In some countries, we see insufficient political commitment to roll out vaccines. This was impacted by the initial lack of political commitment for equitable access to vaccines. In some, we see gaps in operational or financial capacity. And in all, we see vaccine hesitancy driven by misinformation and disinformation.

Safe and effective vaccines are available that provide strong protection against serious illness, hospitalization and death from COVID-19. Billions of people have been vaccinated against COVID-19. Getting vaccinated is one of the most important things a person can do to protect themselves against COVID-19, help end the pandemic and stop new variants emerging.

Take all COVID-19 vaccine doses recommended by your health authority as soon as turn comes, including a booster dose if recommended.

It is still possible to get COVID-19 and spread it to others after being vaccinated, so continue to do everything a person can to keep themselves and others healthy. Continue keeping a safe distance from others and avoiding crowds, wearing a well-fitting mask covering mouth and nose, keeping indoor spaces well ventilated, cleaning hands regularly and covering coughs and sneezes. If a person do get COVID-19 after vaccination, they are more likely to have mild or no symptoms than if they hadn't been vaccinated.

BIBILOGRAPHY

1. Arora S, Saquib S A, Attar N, Pimpale S, Zafar K S, Saluja P, et al. Evaluation of Knowledge And Preparedness Among Indian Dentists During the Current COVID-19 Pandemic: A Cross-Sectional Study. Journal of Multidisciplinary Healthcare 2020;13: 841–854.
2. Cascella M, Rajnik M, Aleem A, et al. Features, Evaluation, and Treatment of Coronavirus (COVID-19) [Updated 2021 Sep 2]. In: StatPearls [Internet]. Treasure Island (FL): StatPearls Publishing; Jan 2021. Doi: https://www.ncbi.nlm.nih.gov/books/NBK554776/#article-52171.s2
3. Bakaeen L G, Masri R, AlTarawneh S, Gracia L T, AlHadidi A, Khamis A H, Hamdan A M, et al. Dentists' knowledge, attitudes, and professional behaviour toward the COVID-19 pandemic: A multisite survey of dentists' perspectives. JADA. 2021;152(1):16-24.
4. Bansal P, Agnihotri A, GuptaA, Singh G, KaurA, Arora R, et al. Emergency preparedness of oral health professionals during COVID-19 pandemic: A knowledge, attitude, and practices study. Indian J Dent Sci 2020;12:137-44.
5. Rana R, Tripathi A, Kumar N, Ganguly NK. A Comprehensive Overview on COVID-19: Future Perspectives. Front. Cell. Infect. Microbiol.2021; 11:744903. doi: 10.3389/fcimb.2021.744903
6. Araf Y, Akter F, Tang Y-d, et al. Omicron variant of SARS-CoV-2: Genomics, transmissibility, and responses to current COVID-19 vaccines. J Med Virol. 2022;94:1825-1832. doi:10.1002/jmv.27588
7. Chams N, Chams S, Badran R, Shams A, Araji A, Raad M. COVID-19: A Multidisciplinary Review. Front. Public Health; 2020: 8:383. doi: 10.3389/fpubh.2020.00383
8. Almaghaslah D, Kandasamy G, Almanasef M, Vasudevan R, Chandramohan S. Review on the coronavirus disease (COVID-19) pandemic: Its outbreak and current status. Int J Clin Pract. 2020;74: e13637. https://doi.org/10.1111/ijcp.13637
9. World Health Organization. Novel coronavirus situation report—2. https://www.who.int/docs/default-source/coronaviruse/ situation-reports/20200122-sitrep-2-2019-ncov.pdf. Accessed February 12, 2020Chen Y, LiuQ, Guo D. Emerging coronaviruses: Genome structure, replication, and pathogenesis. J Med Virol. 2020;92:418–423. DOI: 10.1002/jmv.25681
10. Luka H K H, Lia X, Funga J, Laua S K P, Woo P C Y. Molecular epidemiology, evolution and phylogeny of SARS coronavirus. Infection, Genetics and Evolution 71 2019; 21–30 https://doi.org/10.1016/j.meegid.2019.03.001
11. Zhu N, Zhang D, Wang W, Li X, Yang B, Song J, et al. A Novel Coronavirus from Patients with Pneumonia in China, 2019. N Engl J Med 2020; 382:727-33. DOI: 10.1056/NEJMoa2001017
12. Joost Wiersinga W, Rhodes A, Cheng A C, Peacock S J, Prescott H C. Pathophysiology, Transmission, Diagnosis, and Treatment of Coronavirus Disease 2019 (COVID-19) A Review. JAMA. 2020;324(8):782-793. doi:10.1001/jama.2020.12839
13. Dhama K, Khan S, Tiwari R, Sircar S, Bhat S, Malik YS, Singh KP, Chaicumpa W, Bonilla-Aldana DK, Rodriguez-Morales AJ. 2020. Coronavirus disease 2019 –COVID-19. Clin Microbiol Rev 33:e00028-20. https://doi.org/10 .1128/CMR.00028-20.
14. Harapan H, Itohd N, Yufika A, Winardif W , Keamg S, Te H,et al. Coronavirus disease 2019 (COVID-19): A literature review. Journal of Infection and Public Health 13.2020; 667–673
15. Harapana H, Itohd N, Yufika A, Winardif W , Keamg S, Te H, et al. Coronavirus disease 2019 (COVID-19): A literature review. Journal of Infection and Public Health 13 (2020) 667–673
16. Centers for Disease Control and Prevention. Clinical Spectrum of SARS-CoV-2 Infection. https://www.covid19treatmentguidelines.nih.gov/
17. Tong JY, Wong A, Zhu D, Fastenberg JH, Tham T. The prevalence of olfactory and gustatory dysfunction in COVID-19 patients: a systematic review and meta-analysis. Otolaryngol Head Neck Surg. 2020;163(1):3-11.

https://doi.org/10.1177/0194599820 926473
18. Ambaldhage V, Puttabuddi J, Nunsavath P, Tummuru Y. Taste disorders: a review. J Indian Acad Oral Med Radiol. 2014;26(1):69-76. https://doi.org/10.4103/0972-1363.141864
19. Farid H, Khan M, Jamal S, Ghafoor R. Oral manifestations of Covid-19-A literature review. Rev Med Virol. 2021;e2248. https://doi.org/10.1002/rmv.2248
20. Riad A, Kassem I, Hockova B, Badrah M, Klugar M. Tongue ulcers associated with SARS-CoV-2 infection: a case series. Oral Dis. 2020;00(August):1-3. https://doi.org/10.1111/odi.13635
21. Marzano AV, Cassano N, Genovese G, Moltrasio C, Vena GA. Cutaneous manifestations in patients with COVID-19: a preliminary review of an emerging issue. Br J Dermatol. 2020;183:431-442. https://doi.org/10.1111/bjd.19264
22. Jimenez-Cauhe J, Ortega-Quijano D, Carretero-Barrio I, et al. Erythema multiforme-like eruption in patients with COVID-19 infection: clinical and histological findings. Clin Exp Dermatol. Published online. 2020;45(7):0-2. https://doi.org/10.1111/ced. 14281
23. Martinez-Rojas MA, Vega-Vega O, Bobadilla NA. Is the kidney a target of SARS-CoV-2? Am J Physiol Renal Physiol. 2020 Jun 01;318(6):F1454-F1462. [PMC free article: PMC7303722] [PubMed: 32412303]
24. Gupta A, Madhavan MV, Sehgal K, Nair N, Mahajan S, Sehrawat TS, et al. Extrapulmonary manifestations of COVID-19. Nat Med. 2020 Jul;26(7):1017-1032. [PubMed: 32651579]
25. Hessami A, Shamshirian A, Heydari K, Pourali F, Alizadeh-Navaei R, Moosazadeh M, et al. Cardiovascular diseases burden in COVID-19: Systematic review and meta-analysis. Am J Emerg Med. 2021 Aug;46:382-391. [PMC free article: PMC7561581] [PubMed: 33268238]
26. Coopersmith CM, Antonelli M, Bauer SR, Deutschman CS, Evans LE, Ferrer R, et al. The Surviving Sepsis Campaign: Research Priorities for Coronavirus Disease 2019 in Critical Illness. Crit Care Med. 2021 Apr 01;49(4):598-622. [PubMed: 33591008]
27. Tariq R, Saha S, Furqan F, Hassett L, Pardi D, Khanna S. Prevalence and Mortality of COVID-19 Patients With Gastrointestinal Symptoms: A Systematic Review and Meta-analysis. Mayo Clin Proc. 2020 Aug;95(8):1632-1648. [PMC free article: PMC7284248] [PubMed: 32753138]
28. Xu L, Liu J, Lu M, Yang D, Zheng X. Liver injury during highly pathogenic human coronavirus infections. Liver Int. 2020 May;40(5):998-1004. [PMC free article: PMC7228361] [PubMed: 32170806]
29. Zubair AS, McAlpine LS, Gardin T, Farhadian S, Kuruvilla DE, Spudich S. Neuropathogenesis and Neurologic Manifestations of the Coronaviruses in the Age of Coronavirus Disease 2019: A Review. JAMA Neurol. 2020 Aug 01;77(8):1018-1027. [PMC free article: PMC7484225] [PubMed: 32469387]
30. Siam H B, Nishat N H , Ahmed A, Hossain M S. Stopping the COVID-19 Pandemic: A Review on the Advances of Diagnosis, Treatment, and Control Measures. Journal of Pathogens; 2020:12 https://doi.org/10.1155/2020/9121429
31. US Food and Drug Administration. 2020. Coronavirus disease (COVID-19) Emergency Use Authorization (EUA) information—in vitro diagnostic EUAs. https://www.fda.gov/medical-devices/emergency-situations-medical-devices/emergency-use-authorizations#covid19ivd.
32. Wiersinga WJ, Rhodes A, Cheng AC, Peacock SJ, Prescott HC. Pathophysiology, Transmission, Diagnosis, and Treatment of Coronavirus Disease 2019 (COVID-19): A Review. JAMA. 2020 Aug 25;324(8):782-793. [PubMed: 32648899]
33. Joung J, Ladha A, Saito M, Segel M, Bruneau R, Huang M W,et al. Point-of-care testing for COVID-19 using SHERLOCK diagnostics. MedRxiv;2020. Available online at: https://doi.org/10.1101/2020.05.04.20091231
34. Al-Tawfiq J A ,Memish Z A. "Diagnosis of SARS-CoV-2 infection based on CT scan vs RT-PCR: reflecting on experience from MERS-CoV," Journal of Hospital Infection.2020; vol. 105: no. 2, pp. 154-155
35. Wu D, Wu T, Liu Q, Yang Z.",The SARS-CoV-2 outbreak: what we know," International Journal of Infectious

Diseases.2020; vol. 94: pp. 44–48

36. Yan L, Zhang H T, Xiao Y,Wang M, Guo Y, Sun C, et al. "Prediction of criticality in patients with severe Covid-19 infection using three clinical features: a machine learning-based prognostic model with clinical data in Wuhan,". MedRxiv;2020. Available online at: https://doi.org/10.1101/2020.02.27.20028027
37. Henrina J, Cahyo I, Putra S, Lawrensia S, Handoyono Q F, Cahyadi A . Coronavirus Disease of 2019: a Mimicker of Dengue Infection? SN Comprehensive Clinical Medicine (2020) 2:1109–1119. Available online at: https://doi.org/10.1007/s42399-020-00364-3
38. Yao X, Ye F, Zhang M, Cui C, Huang B, Niu P, et al. In vitro antiviral activity and projection of optimized dosing design of hydroxychloroquine for the treatment of severe acute respiratory syndrome coronavirus 2 (SARS-CoV2). Clin Infect Dis. 2020;237. doi: 10.1093/cid/ciaa237
39. Boulware DR, Pullen MF, Bangdiwala AS, Pastick KA, Lofgren SM, Okafor EC, et al. A randomized trial of hydroxychloroquine as postexposure prophylaxis for Covid-19. N Engl J Med.2020; NEJMoa:2016638. doi: 10.1056/NEJMoa,2016638
40. U. S., Food, and Drug Administration. Coronavirus (COVID-19) Update: FDA Revokes Emergency Use Authorization for Chloroquine and Hydroxychloroquine. 2020; Available online at: https://www.fda.gov/news-events/press-announcements/coronavirus-covid-19-update-fdarevokes-emergency-use-authorization-chloroquine-and (accessed June 15, 2020).
41. Amsden GW. Anti-inflammatory effects of macrolides–an underappreciated benefit in the treatment of community-acquired respiratory tract infections and chronic inflammatory pulmonary conditions? J Antimicrob Chemother. 2005; 55:10–21. doi: 10.1093/jac/dkh519
42. Groneberg DA, Poutanen SM, Low DE, Lode H, Welte T, Zabel P. Treatment and vaccines for severe acute respiratory syndrome. Lancet Infect Dis. 2005;5:147–55. doi: 10.1016/S1473-3099(05)70022-0
43. Cao B, Wang Y, Wen D, Liu W, Wang J, Fan G, et al. A trial of lopinavirritonavir in adults hospitalized with severe Covid-19. N Engl J Med. 2020; 382:1787–99. doi: 10.1056/NEJMoa2001282
44. Dong L, Hu S, Gao J. Discovering drugs to treat coronavirus disease 2019 (COVID-19). Drug Discov Ther. 2020; 14:58–60. doi: 10.5582/ddt.2020.01012
45. Caly L, Druce JD, Catton MG, Jans DA, Wagstaff KM. The FDA-approved drug ivermectin inhibits the replication of SARS-CoV-2 in vitro. Antiviral Res. 2020; 178:104787. doi: 10.1016/j.antiviral.2020.104787
46. Horby P, Lim WS, Emberson J, Mafham M,Bell J,Linsell L, et al. Effect of Dexamethasone in Hospitalized Patients With COVID-19 – Preliminary Report. 2020. Available online at: https://www.medrxiv.org/content/10. 1101/2020.06.22.20137273v1.full.pdf (accessed June 23, 2020)
47. Duan K, Liu B, Li C, Zhang H, Yu T, Qu J, et al. Effectiveness of convalescent plasma therapy in severe COVID-19 patients. Proc Natl Acad Sci USA. 2020; 117:9490–6. doi: 10.1073/pnas.2004168117
48. . U. S., and Food Drug Administration. Investigational COVID-19 convalescent plasma - emergency INDs. 2020; Available online at: https:// www.fda.gov/vaccines-blood-biologics/investigational-new-drug-ind-ordevice-exemption-ide-process-cber/recommendations-investigationalcovid-19-convalescent-plasma (accessed April 13 2020)
49. Thachil J, Tang N, Gando S, Falanga A, Cattaneo M, Levi M, et al. ISTH interim guidance on recognition and management of coagulopathy in COVID-19. J Thromb Haemost. 2020; 18:1023–26. doi: 10.1111/jth.1 4810
50. Boretti A, Banik BK. Intravenous vitamin C for reduction of cytokines storn in acute respiratory distress syndrome. Pharma Nutr. 2020; 12:100190. doi: 10.1016/j.phanu.2020.100190
51. Fowler AA, Truwit JD, Hite RD, Morris PE, DeWilde C, Priday, A. Effect of vitamin C. JAMA. 2019; 322:1261–70. doi: 10.1001/jama.2019.11825
52. Te Velthuis AJ, Van Den Worm SH, Sims AC, Baric RS, Snijder EJ, Van Hemert MJ. Zn(2+) inhibits coronavirus and arterivirus RNA polymerase activity in vitro and zinc ionophores block the replication of these viruses in cell culture. PLoS Pathog. 2010; 6:e1001176. doi: 10.1371/journal.ppat.1001176

53. ClinicalTrials.gov. A Study of Hydroxychloroquine, Vitamin C, Vitamin D, and Zinc for the Prevention of COVID-19 Infection (HELPCOVID-19). 2020; Available online at: https://clinicaltrials.gov/ct2/show/NCT04335084 (accessed June 23, 2020).
54. ClinicalTrials.gov. The COVID-19 Symptom Motelukast Trial (COSMO).2020. Available online at: https://clinicaltrials.gov/ct2/show/NCT04389411 (accessed June 23, 2020).
55. ClinicalTrials.gov. Safety and Immunogenicity Study of 2019-nCoV Vaccine (mRNA-1273) for Prophylaxis SARS CoV-2 Infection (COVID-19).2020. Available online at: https://clinicaltrials.gov/ct2/show/NCT04283461 (accessed April 16, 2020).
56. Tran, K., Cimon, K., Severn, M., Pessoa-Silva, C. L., & Conly, J. (2012). Aerosol generating procedures and risk of transmission of acute respiratory infections to healthcare workers: a systematic review. PloS one, 7(4). Available online at: https://www.ncbi.nlm.nih.gov/pmc/articles/PMC3338532/
57. Infection prevention and control during health care when novel coronavirus (nCoV) infection is suspected. Interim Guidance. Geneva: World Health Organization; 2020.
58. Standard precautions in health care. Geneva: World Health Organization; 2007 (accessed 2 April 2020).
59. Infection prevention and control of epidemic-and pandemic-prone acute respiratory infections in health care. Geneva: World Health Organization; 2014 (accessed 27 February 2020).
60. World Health Organization. Rational use of personal protective equipment for coronavirus disease (COVID-19) and considerations during severe shortages Interim guidance; 6 April 2020.
61. World Health Organization. How to put on and how to remove personal protective equipment(PPE). 24 January 2015.
62. AIIMS/ ICMR-COVID-19 National Task Force/ Joint Monitoring Group (Dte.GHS) Ministry of Health & Family Welfare, Government of India. CLINICAL GUIDANCE FOR MANAGEMENT OF ADULT COVID-19 PATIENTS. (Revised on 14/01/2022)
63. World Health Organization. Coronavirus disease (Covid 19): vaccines. 17 May 2022
64. World Health Organization. The Oxford/AstraZeneca (ChAdOx1-S [recombinant] vaccine) COVID-19 vaccine: what you need to know. *[Updated: 13 June 2022]*
65. World Health Organization. The Bharat Biotech BBV152 COVAXIN vaccine against COVID-19: What you need to know. [Updated 10 June 2022]
66. Silva Andrade B, Siqueira S, De Assis Soares W R, De Souza Rangel F, Santos N O, Dos Santos Freitas A, et al. Long-COVID and Post-COVID Health Complications: An Up-to-Date Review on Clinical Conditions and Their Possible Molecular Mechanisms. Viruses 2021, 13, 700. Available online at: https://doi.org/10.3390/v13040700
67. Shahmirzaei S, Moghadasi A N. Association Of Covid-19 And Acute Disseminated Encephalomyelitis (Adem) In The Absence Of Pulmonary Involvement. Autoimmun. 2021;Rev. 20 (3), 102753. doi: 10.1016/j.autrev.2021.102753
68. Ramos-Casals M, Brito-Zerón P, Mariette X. Systemic And OrganSpecific Immune-Related Manifestations Of Covid-19. Nat. Rev. Rheumatol.2021; 17: 315–332. doi: 10.1038/s41584-021-00608-z
69. Velez J C , Caza T, Larsen C P. Covan Is The New HIVAN: The Re-Emergence Of Collapsing Glomerulopathy With COVID-19. Nat. Rev. Nephrol.2020; 16, 565–567. doi: 10.1038/s41581-020-0332-3
70. Garg D, Muthu V, Sehgal I S, Ramachandran R, Kaur H, Bhalla A, et al. Coronavirus Disease (Covid-19) Associated Mucormycosis (Cam): Case Report And Systematic Review Of Literature. Mycopathologia .2021;186 (2): 289–298. doi: 10.1007/s11046-021-00528-2
71. Lehrer R I, Howard D H, Sypherd P S, Edwards J E, Segal G P, Winston D J . Mucormycosis. Ann. Internal Med.1980; 93: 93–108. doi: 10.7326/0003-4819-93-1-93
72. Richardson M D, Rautemaa-Richardson R. Biotic Environments Supporting The Persistence Of Clinically Relevant Mucormycetes. J. Fungi 2020;6 (1): 4. doi: 10.3390/jof6010004

73. Spellberg B, Edwards J J, Ibrahim A. Novel Perspectives On Mucormycosis: Pathophysiology, Presentation, And Management. Clin. Microbiol.2005; Rev. 18: 556–569. doi: 10.1128/CMR.18.3.556-569.2005
74. brahim A S, Spellberg B, Walsh T J, Kontoyiannis D P. Pathogenesis Of Mucormycosis. Clin. Infect. Dis.2012; 54; S16–S22. doi: 10.1093/ cid/cir865
75. Skiada A, Pavleas I, Drogari-Apiranthitou M. Epidemiology And Diagnosis Of Mucormycosis: An Update. J. Fungi.2020;6 (4): 265. doi: 10.3390/ jof6040265
76. Castrejón-Pérez A D, Welsh E C, Miranda I, Ocampo-Candiani J, Welsh O. Cutaneous Mucormycosis. Anais Brasileiros Dermatol.2017; 92: 304–311. doi: 10.1590/abd1806-4841.20176614
77. Serris, A., Danion, F., and Lanternier, F. (2019). Disease Entities In Mucormycosis. J. Fungi 5, 23. doi: 10.3390/ jof5010023
78. Mehta S, Pandey A. Rhino-Orbital Mucormycosis Associated With Covid-19. Cureus. 2020;12 (9): e10726. doi: 10.7759/cureus.10726
79. Spellberg B, Kontoyiannis D P, Fredricks D, Morris M I, Perfect J R, ChinHong P V, et al. Risk Factors For Mortality In Patients With Mucormycosis. Med.2012; Mycol 50:611–618. doi: 10.3109/13693786.2012.669502

Contents

Printed by Libri Plureos GmbH in Hamburg,
Germany

9 798888 055823